Managing Information Resources for Insurance

Managing Information Resources for Insurance

CPCU 7—Management

Leonard J. Watson, CPCU,CIC
Director of Curriculum
American Institute for CPCU

First Edition • 1998

American Institute for CPCU
Malvern, Pennsylvania

First Edition • Third Printing • May 2001

Library of Congress Catalog Number: 98-71637
International Standard Book Number: 0-89463-083-0

Printed in Canada

Dedication

This text is dedicated to the memory of the late Dr. James Gatza, CPCU, AIM, vice president of the American Institute for CPCU and the Insurance Institute of America.

For over twenty-five years, Jim was responsible for the Management course of the CPCU curriculum as well as other aspects of management and supervisory education at the American Institute for CPCU and the Insurance Institute of America (IIA). He coauthored two texts, *Decision Making in Administration* and *Managing Automated Activities*.

A native of Buffalo, NY, Jim received his bachelor's and master's degrees from the State University of New York at Buffalo. After serving five years as an electronic warfare officer in the United States Air Force, Jim received his doctoral degree from Harvard Business School in 1965. Jim spent five years on the faculty of Villanova University, including three years as chairman of the Department of Management, before joining the Institutes. For many years, he directed the IIA Associate in Management program and the IIA Program in Supervisory Management. As program director, he developed the Associate in Automation Management program and remained responsible for it until the time of his death. Jim also directed the Institutes' Advanced Executive Education program, co-sponsored by the Wharton School of the University of Pennsylvania. He had a number of Institute-wide marketing responsibilities and served as a frequent speaker at insurance industry meetings.

Foreword

The American Institute for Chartered Property Casualty Underwriters, the Insurance Institute of America, and the Insurance Institute for Applied Ethics are independent, nonprofit, educational organizations serving the needs of the property and liability insurance business. The Institutes develop a wide range of programs—curricula, study materials, and examinations—in response to the educational requirements of various elements of the business.

The American Institute confers the Chartered Property Casualty Underwriter (CPCU®) professional designation on those who meet the Institute's experience, ethics, and examination requirements.

The Insurance Institute of America offers associate designations and certificate programs in the following technical and managerial disciplines:

Accredited Adviser in Insurance (AAI®)
Associate in Automation Management (AAM®)
Associate in Claims (AIC)
Associate in Fidelity and Surety Bonding (AFSB)
Associate in Insurance Accounting and Finance (AIAF)
Associate in Insurance Services (AIS)
Associate in Loss Control Management (ALCM®)
Associate in Management (AIM)
Associate in Marine Insurance Management (AMIM®)
Associate in Personal Insurance (API)
Associate in Premium Auditing (APA®)
Associate in Reinsurance (ARe)
Associate in Research and Planning (ARP®)
Associate in Surplus Lines Insurance (ASLI)
Associate in Underwriting (AU)
Insurance Regulation
Program in General Insurance
Program in Supervisory Management
Introduction to Property and Liability Insurance

Introduction to Claims
Introduction to Risk Management
Introduction to Underwriting
Writing at Work
Focus Series
    Topical Presentations—CE Credit

The Center for Advanced Risk Management Education (CARME), a division of the American Institute for CPCU and the Insurance Institute of America, serves as the focal point for the Institutes' risk management programs:

    Associate in Risk Management (ARM)
    Risk Management for Health Care Organizations

The Insurance Institute for Applied Ethics was established in 1995 to heighten awareness of the pervasiveness of ethical decision making in insurance and to explore ways to raise the level of ethical behavior among parties to the insurance contract. The Ethics Institute sponsors seminars and workshops on the role of ethics in the insurance transaction. It also identifies and funds practical research projects on ethics-related topics and publishes the findings. In addition, it produces booklets, newsletters, and videotapes on ethics issues.

The Institutes began publishing textbooks in 1976 to help students meet the national examination standards. Since that time, we have produced more than ninety individual textbook volumes. Despite the vast differences in the subjects and purposes of these volumes, they all have much in common. First, each book is specifically designed to increase knowledge and develop skills that can improve job performance and help students achieve the educational objectives of the course for which it is assigned. Second, all of the manuscripts of our texts are widely reviewed before publication, by both insurance business practitioners and members of the academic community. In addition, all of our texts and course guides also reflect the work of Institute staff members. These writing or editing duties are seen as an integral part of their professional responsibilities, and no one earns a royalty based on the sale of our texts. We have proceeded in this way to avoid even the appearance of any conflict of interests. Finally, the revisions of our texts often incorporate improvements suggested by students and course leaders.

We welcome criticisms of and suggestions for improving our publications. It is only with such constructive comments that we can hope to improve the quality of our study materials. Please direct any comments you may have on this text to the Curriculum Department of the Institutes.

Lawrence G. Brandon, CPCU, AIM, ARM
Chairman

Preface

Managing Information Resources for Insurance is a new book for CPCU 7 introduced in 1998, replacing *Managing Information Resources,* which was published in 1995. This text continues the objective of its predecessor to emphasize the sources and use of information rather than the technology that facilitates access.

Technology continues to evolve rapidly, becoming more accessible to individuals with relatively little technical proficiency. Anticipating that technology will continue to be transparent to those that depend on it to record and access data, this book examines common needs and uses for information in the insurance business. It forms three assignments within CPCU 7, which examines a broad range of management issues. This book explores how the insurer and agency management processes use technology to improve operational efficiency and customer service, increasing the depth of information available to those who work in the insurance business and giving them greater access to financial and statistical data for analysis and regulatory compliance.

Institute texts benefit from the insight and critical review of many individuals. Of special help in the preparation of this book was review provided by Michael W. Elliott, CPCU, AIAF; James F. Fryer, Ed.D., CPCU; James J. Markham, J.D., CPCU, AIC, AIAF; and Peter Tyler, CPCU, AU, ARM, AAM.

The technology that allows us to effectively manage information resources will continue to change, and future editions of this book will respond to those changes.

Leonard J. Watson

Contents

Chapter 1

Information Needs in Insurance

Insurance is a mechanism for transferring the financial consequences of loss. Insurers are willing to accept that transfer partly because they can accurately assess the probable frequency and severity of losses when they have a sufficient pool of data describing similar risks exposed to similar perils. Insurers gain confidence in their ability to assess losses when they understand the implications of many different facts. When facts, or **data**, are carefully compiled and ordered so that they add value to decision making, they are called **information.**

> **Data** are a collection of facts, statistics, numbers, or other details. **Information** is the carefully constructed compilation of data in a clear and ordered format that contributes to decision making. An **information system** is a network for providing information that management needs to make decisions.

This text reviews the types of data insurers collect and examines how the data are used to develop useful information. An **information system** is a network for providing information that management needs to make decisions, whether employees provide that service by manually evaluating data or by using an electronic source. This text assumes that students are familiar with the common technological vocabulary currently used in the insurance business by underwriting, marketing, administrative, actuarial, and claim personnel. It does not emphasize the technology of electronic data manipulation, but instead identifies the types of data that are most important to insurance practitioners. It also explains why information based on that data is important and how that information is used to help insurers meet their objectives and obligations.

Uses of Information

Senior managers of hypothetical Outstanding Insurance Company (OIC) have year-end earned premium data for commercial auto liability products of $400 million in 1996, $420 million in 1997, and $450 million in 1998 (see Exhibit 1-1). In the same years, commercial auto liability losses were $260 million, $270 million, and $320 million, respectively. Earned premium grew 5 percent between the first and the second years and 7 percent between the second and the third years. Losses grew 3.8 percent between the first and the second years and 18.5 between the second and the third years. The loss ratios for each of these years were 65 percent, 64.3 percent, and 71.1 percent, respectively. These are facts, or items of data. Similarly, the investment return rates of 9 percent in 1996, 12 percent in 1997, and 19 percent in 1998 are facts.

Exhibit 1-1
OIC Three Year Results—Commercial Auto

	1996	1997	1998
Earned Premium	$400	$420 (+5%)	$450 (+7%)
Incurred Losses	$260	$270 (+3.8%)	$320 (+18.5%)
Loss Ratio	65%	64.3%	71.1%
Investment Returns	9%	12%	19%

Interpreting facts converts raw data into information. A preliminary analysis of OIC's raw data reveals that premium is rising at an increasing rate. Losses are also increasing, and, in the most recent year, losses increased significantly more than premium increased, a sign that the loss ratio deteriorated in 1998. The 1998 loss ratio supports that observation. Fortunately for OIC, investment returns have also increased. The 19 percent return in 1998 could offset much of the 18.5 percent increase in losses that occurred between 1997 and 1998. In any case, the numbers alone are meaningless; data like the facts in Exhibit 1-1 must be properly interpreted before they can be used in an insurer's decision-making process. Before they are converted into information, data are subject to different, possibly conflicting, interpretations; for example, the increasing losses might be the result of a catastrophe, or they might simply reflect inadequate pricing or marginal underwriting practices.

Experienced insurance professionals are not content just to produce profitable results. They monitor data about premium, losses, expenses, and many other measures of insurer performance to identify results that deviate from expected results. The causes of deviations are then evaluated using a range of data sources available to insurer management. Insurers manage information resources by using data to develop valuable information about business operations so that they can achieve their objectives.

Insurers use data and information to satisfy the demands of the following groups:

- Regulatory authorities
- Owners and other (non-employee) stakeholders, including policyholders
- Management and employees

Regulatory Authorities

Regulatory authorities are charged by state statute with the responsibility of protecting the insurance industry's policyholders from insurer financial insolvency and from unreasonable business practices. Much of an insurer's data collection activity exists to satisfy the information requirements of regulatory authorities. Regulators require that insurers provide two categories of data: statistical and financial.

Statistical Data

State regulators are interested in knowing about the underwriting and marketing practices of each insurer operating in their state. For example, states require the following categories of data with respect to property insurance risks:

- State
- Territory
- City
- County
- Rating classification
- Construction type or category
- Public protection classification or code
- Deductible amount and whether flat or percentage
- Insurance amount
- Year of construction

Insurers record data for data categories such as those for each line of business they write and submit statistical reports to independent statistical agencies like Insurance Services Office (ISO) and the National Association of Independent Insurers (NAII). Those organizations assemble, or aggregate, the information provided by each individual insurer, by line of business, and submit detailed reports to the states.

In addition to data for written premium, states require detailed data such as the following:

- Number of written exposures (exposure units)
- Number and value of paid losses
- Number and value of reserves for unpaid losses

The states determine which data insurers must collect and how frequently they must submit reports. States require insurers to report statistical data on paper, electronically, or both. States also receive industry data from statistical reporting agencies that collect data from multiple insurers in a uniform format. Because statistical reporting agencies can compile many insurers' results, states find that information useful for benchmarking and comparison purposes. States can also use data from statistical reporting agencies for much of their information about the financial performance of specific insurers. Insurers submit data to statistical reporting agencies, which compare loss experience, premium levels, and profitability with those of other insurers. The detailed statistical data required by state regulators and statistical reporting agencies also help insurers to manage their results.

Using Data To Improve Customer Service

Because regulators define and require substantial statistical detail, insurers sometimes accept that level of detail as sufficient for their own analytic purposes. Consequently, those insurers might fail to consider additional types of data that they could voluntarily collect and analyze and that would give them information to help them improve their customer service.

For example, states typically require insurers to record claim details. One item of data required in some states is the number of days between a first report of loss to the insurer and the date on which the insurer's claim representative first contacts the insured. Because this item of data is captured and analyzed, insurers can use it to provide information about how promptly customers receive claim service. It can then be used to improve that service.

In contrast, regulators typically do not require insurers to capture data about how long it takes to process an application for a new policy. Consequently, insurers might not have data that could be used to provide information about the timeliness with which they handle requests for coverage. If the information revealed application processing time that management considered excessive, management could take action to improve the performance of that task. If, on the other hand, the information revealed that the insurer consistently delivered extremely fast service, management could use that information as a marketing tool.

Portfolio analysis is the process of identifying, collecting, sorting, and analyzing data about a group of risks.

Since electronic systems process so much of an insurer's activity, an insurer can establish procedures to identify and capture more data than regulators require. Greater amounts and types of data can be sorted and analyzed to provide information that would help improve the organization's understanding of its results. When organizations use comprehensive data collection and analysis processes for a group of risks, they are performing **portfolio analysis**, sometimes called book of business analysis. Insurers with high levels of portfolio analysis skill may be able to identify opportunities and problems more rapidly than insurers that are less skilled in evaluating data and interpreting information. That can improve their competitiveness, increase profits, and help define market niches in which higher levels of information are needed to achieve underwriting and pricing objectives.

Financial Data

Besides requiring insurers to provide statistical data, regulators also require insurers to demonstrate their financial solvency by submitting company financial data. Financial data are also important to the insurer's owners and other stakeholders. Investors, investment analysts, federal securities regulators, creditors, agents, policyholders, and employees all have an interest in an insurer's overall financial strength and are therefore interested in its financial data.

Accounting Procedures: SAP Versus GAAP

Two types of accounting procedures are used in the insurance industry (and are examined in substantial detail in CPCU 8). The accounting procedures required by insurance regulators and statistical data collection organizations are called statutory accounting principles (SAP). They emphasize financial data related to insurer solvency. Insurers also present their financial data according to generally accepted accounting principles (GAAP), as do most other noninsurance businesses.

SAP presents the financial condition of an insurer in a more conservative fashion than GAAP. For example, SAP requires insurers to immediately recognize expenses when a policy is issued. GAAP requires the matching of expenses as the policy period elapses; that is, whatever costs an insurer incurs by issuing an insurance policy are spread out over the entire policy period. Insurers provide their financial data using SAP so that they can satisfy the solvency analysis needs of regulators and so that their performance can be compared with the results of other insurers. Insurers also provide their financial data using GAAP for most management purposes, for the Securities and Exchange Commission (SEC), and to facilitate comparisons of their results with the results of noninsurance businesses. The information derived from the GAAP data is particularly important for owners, who compare changes in the insurer's assets, liabilities, and profits with similar data for other investment options.

The following data are typically included in an insurer's financial reporting:

- Fixed maturities (long-term investments and debt obligations)
- Equity securities (long-term investments)
- Cash and short-term securities
- Investment income accrued
- Premium balances receivable
- Deferred acquisition costs
- Real estate
- Furniture and equipment
- Loss reserves
- Loss adjustment expense reserves
- Unearned premium reserves
- Excess of statutory reserves over statement
- Federal income taxes (current and deferred)
- Common stock (of the insurer for stock companies)
- Additional paid-in capital
- Unrealized capital gains
- Retained earnings
- Shareholder equity
- Premiums written
- Increase in unearned premium reserves
- Premiums earned

- Investment income
- Losses
- Amortization of deferred acquisition costs
- Investment expenses
- General and administrative expenses
- Dividends to policyholders (for mutual insurers)

- Realized investment losses (net of taxes)
- Retained earnings (beginning of year)
- Required addition to loss reserves
- Dividends to shareholders

How these data are used to analyze the financial performance of the insurer is beyond the scope of this chapter. However, the extent of this list demonstrates how an insurer's financial record keeping and reporting requirements can satisfy many interested users.

Owners and Other Stakeholders

Financial data represent one type of information that owners and other stakeholders (including policyholders) need, but they are also concerned about how well the organization is operating. The information produced when data have been sorted and interpreted to help owners and other stakeholders understand how well an organization is operating is called operational information. The following are among the groups of owners and other stakeholders interested in operational information:

- Stockholders (and other owners)
- Policyholders
- Claimants
- Agents and brokers

Stockholders

Stockholders evaluate both statistical and financial information to assess whether their investment expectations are being met. To accomplish this evaluation, they review information contained in the annual and quarterly reports to stockholders, the detailed insurance department financial records filings, and investment prospectuses. Stockholders also compare the performance of the insurer's stock over time with other similar stocks (or to the stock market in general) and ratings and evaluations performed and summarized by rating organizations such as A.M. Best's and Standard & Poor.

The availability of operating results from different insurers also affects expectations of owners. If some insurers consistently produce returns on equity of 20 percent or better, directors, representing the expectations of stockholders, are likely to expect their organizations to perform equally well.

Insurer management is typically sensitive to the possible reactions of stockholders to reported financial results because the support of these investors is crucial to the insurer's continuing financial stability. Insurers try to anticipate possible negative reaction to reported results and to include explanations with results reports in documents like the annual report and the prospectus. Similarly, insurers explain deviations from expected results to members of the board of directors at quarterly board meetings.

Stockholders are increasingly holding members of boards of directors accountable for the results of their organizations. Because most directors of insurance companies have experience with comprehensive data collection and analysis systems in other businesses, they expect insurers to use similar systems. Insurer senior managers try to demonstrate to their boards of directors that they are using information to maximize return on stockholder investment.

Corporate directors also understand the importance of effectively managing information in achieving results. Directors have high expectations for an insurer's ability to collect, analyze, and use information in setting rates and defining underwriting practices.

Policyholders

Policyholders expect their insurer to respond to a range of information demands. Initially, they want quick responses to questions about coverage and price. They also expect prompt responses to requests for policy changes. In addition, they expect rapid responses to requests for proof of insurance coverage (for compliance with state compulsory auto insurance laws, protection of lienholder/mortgagee interests, and evidence of workers compensation compliance with state employer–employee statutes). Policyholders also expect the accurate, understandable, and timely handling of premium bills. Of particular importance to policyholders is an insurer's ability to verify coverage information when a claim is presented. Meeting these policyholder demands requires ready access to policyholder information by agents, customer service representatives, and claim personnel.

In addition to policyholder information, insurance customers want to know that their insurer is performing sufficiently well to continue providing the expected level of service. One way policyholders assess performance is by the general information they receive about the insurer. Product advertising and publicity for community involvement are two examples of how insurers make general information available to the public. Agents, brokers, and customer service personnel also provide their customers information about the insurer when they describe its service capability, reputation for quality products, and reliable handling of claims.

For stock insurance companies, the annual report to stockholders is a more formal approach to describing insurer performance. Although mutual insurers have no stockholders, they also produce a summary of performance, called an annual report to policyholders. An annual report uses selected data to provide information about the company's results. It typically includes the following information for the company as a whole as of the end of a calendar year:

- Premium
- Losses
- Expenses for adjusting losses
- Administrative expenses
- Profit or loss
- Investment income
- Dividends
- Taxes

The summary of operating results in the annual report is typically accompanied by an explanation of the financial information. The report also provides information about the place and time of the annual meeting of directors and policyholders as well as a list of the company's major officers. Besides making the annual report available to policyholders, insurers generally distribute copies to their primary agents and brokers, who often use selected information from the annual report to assist in their marketing efforts.

Claimants

Although insurers typically have no information about claimants before a loss occurs, claim representatives accumulate a substantial amount of data during the investigation of a claim. Furthermore, claimants are frequently represented by counsel, who demand prompt attention to their requests for information. Whether or not claimants are represented, the insurer should investigate and settle losses promptly. That obligation requires the insurer to maintain accurate records of the following:

- The claimant's statements
- Dates and times of contacts with the claimant

- Initial and subsequent explanations of the claim process to the claimant
- Appropriate nonwaiver agreements and proofs of loss (if needed)
- Loss details
- Facts developed during the claim investigation
- The claim-handling process
- Reserves
- Coverage evaluation
- The decision-making process
- The final decision
- The settlement

Besides being important to claimants and their representatives, information developed in the claim process is used to monitor the performance of the claim department and to assess compliance with insurer claim guidelines and regulator requirements for prompt investigation and settlement. Initial reserves, reserve adjustments, and payments are also required for both statutory and financial reporting.

Disputes sometimes arise over coverage or settlement amounts, particularly in claims involving allegations of insured liability. In these situations especially, the information contained in a claim file (whether recorded on paper or in electronic form) is important for determining whether the insurer complied with expected claim-handling practices. The insurer's failure to produce information that demonstrates compliance with accepted claim-handling standards can result in regulatory fines as well as a weakened claim defense.

Agents and Brokers

Besides being interested in information about the financial strength of insurers, agents and brokers (together, often called producers) are interested in information about the policies that they sell and service. Since most producers depend on sales for their compensation and since sales are typically measured in the annual premiums of policies, producers are particularly interested in information about premium. Insurers can provide producers with premium data by line of business, customer, customer location, sales representative, geographic location or state, commission level, policy effective date, renewal date, or many other items that might benefit the producer.

Such data are often sorted and evaluated by insurer marketing or underwriting personnel and sent to producers in monthly paper reports, frequently containing the insurer's analysis of the data. Reports typically contain results for the most recent month, the year-to-date totals, and comparisons with prior years.

Some reports also provide results over the six or twelve months before the date of the report to reveal the effects of seasonal differences or unusually high or low short-term results. Many insurers provide their producers with premium data by electronic means, either by electronically transmitting the data to producers or by arranging on-line access to insurer data files directly from the producers' computers.

Commissions usually constitute the majority of producer compensation, but contingency payments or bonuses based on profitability are also common. Consequently, producers want to receive information about losses and loss reserves so that they can assess the probability of receiving such additional compensation. Producers sometimes also assist insurers, particularly with commercial customers, in developing additional loss details when loss amounts or claim frequencies are unusual. As with premiums, insurers carefully monitor loss and reserve data for other reasons and typically include claim data with the premium information they distribute to producers. As with premium data, insurer marketing and underwriting personnel often analyze claim data at the producer level to identify trends that might require discussion with the producer.

Producer commissions represent a significant portion of the insurer's total expenses. Since insurers collect detailed expense data, they can usually report detailed commission information to producers. Although producers typically monitor their commissions independently of the insurer report, the commission data from the insurer provide information with which producers can verify their assessment of commission amounts. Insurer-prepared commission summaries usually accompany the premium and loss information produced on a monthly and year-to-date basis.

Management and Employees

Among those who use insurer information, perhaps no one uses it more frequently than those who work in the insurer's operations. They are responsible for implementing and modifying the procedures required to process insurance applications, produce policy forms, generate bills, collect premiums, and adjust losses. The insurer's producers, underwriters, customer service personnel, claim representatives, and managers identify needed data and record the data either electronically or manually. They also organize data, defining information they can use to achieve the organization's objectives.

Insurers depend on the effective interaction of the following:

- Producers and marketers—to identify and assess the qualifications of prospective insureds

- Underwriters and customer service specialists—to verify risk acceptability and adequacy of pricing and to keep policy information up to date
- Rating and processing—to correctly rate and issue policies
- Administrative support departments—to assemble policy forms and declarations correctly
- Billing and accounting—to bill for and collect premiums due
- Management and portfolio analysts—to monitor results and to identify problems and opportunities
- Claim personnel—to determine coverage correctly, to assess damages accurately, and to settle losses

Information Processing Cycle

The information processing cycle follows four steps:

1. Collect raw data defined as important
2. Classify the data according to date received and intended use
3. Transform the data into needed information useful for business reasons
4. Produce reports summarizing results

The design of any information-gathering system, whether electronic or manual, must first consider what uses of information are required. Manual insurance forms are designed to collect data required to comply with the contractual promises of the insurance contract. Most insurer applications were designed to collect data that could be retrieved and sorted to produce information about the insurance provided. Whether information is needed for statistical, financial, or operational evaluation, insurer management must collect data, classify the data into groups of similar types, perform specific processes on the data, and establish a record of the process.

Collection

Collection is the logical gathering and recording of raw data from source documents such as invoices, purchase orders, time records, applications for insurance, requests for coverage changes, claim reports, and payments. For example, a producer begins the data collection process when completing an application for workers compensation insurance. Among the data that producers collect are the insured's name, address, locations, and type of operation; employee names; types of jobs performed; and payroll amounts that apply to each classification of employee. The producer may collect data on a paper application or by making entries into a computer data file, which might be stored in the producer's office, transmitted to the insurer, or both. If insurers or state regulations require policyholders to sign an original paper application, a computer-prepared version of the application can be printed for that purpose.

A **field** is a space into which data items are entered on a source document (such as a new business insurance application), or on the corresponding computer screens for an electronic source document.

Data entry operators use source documents to record raw data in a database. If the original data collection process occurs electronically, the data entry function can be accomplished simultaneously with data collection.

Insurers design preprinted forms and computer screen formats to collect needed data in the most efficient manner. The spaces into which data are entered on a new business insurance application, or on the corresponding computer screens for an electronic application, are called **fields**, or transaction fields. The space provided for the name of a policyholder is an example of a field on an application. Other fields include such data items as transaction code (new business, endorsement, cancellation, or renewal) policy number, effective or expiration date, and coverage codes.

The purpose of collecting all of the required data for an application and entering the data into a computer is to decide coverage eligibility and price. Whether an individual or a computer program makes the eligibility and pricing decisions, some action must be taken after all the data have been collected. Especially in personal lines, insurers are increasingly transferring a significant portion of their underwriting and pricing decisions and subsequent action to computer programs. For a new application, that action might include comparing data with a set of risk characteristics (screening), referring the application to an underwriter, calculating premium due, creating a billing record, producing policy documents, or mailing coverage verification to a lienholder or mortgagee. Before the system can perform any of those functions, it must classify the completed transaction.

Classification is a means to organize data according to the system's requirements.

Classification

Information systems, whether manual, electronic, or some combination, are processes that organize data. How the collected data are organized affects the usefulness of the information derived from the data. To help people recognize how data can best be used, systems designers try to establish a pattern for processing data so that systems users can focus on using the data rather than on how the data are input and processed.

Transaction validation edits are a comparison of the data input from a source document with predefined parameters to determine whether the data are in a proper form or value.

After data are recorded from a source document to an electronic file, the system must do something with the data. First, it performs **transaction validation edits** to determine whether the data provided in a particular field match the system's definition of the requirements for that particular type of transaction. For example, an insurer might decide to distinguish between new business and policy renewal transactions. It might wish to make that distinction for many reasons, such as applying one set of pricing or underwriting guidelines to renewals and another set to new policies.

To distinguish between source documents for new and renewal policies, the insurer might define an input code of "N" for new and "R" for renewal. Producers and underwriters would then be expected to include that code in the appropriate field on any source document they create. Insurer management would want to verify that such coding on the source document was correct. An underwriter could be assigned to search the insurer's customer database for customer names and addresses every time a source document is input.

That same task could be accomplished electronically. The system would electronically check all of the company's policyholder files to locate a match with exact or similar names and addresses using the source document fields for name and address. If that verification process confirms the code contained in the "N" versus "R" field on the source document, the system would continue processing the data from the source document. If the validation edit fails to validate the code indicated on the source document, then the source document would be referred to an underwriter for investigation, or an electronic message would notify an underwriter of the discrepancy.

Both manual and electronic systems can also compare the codes in different fields to verify the compatibility of different data items. For example, an application for auto insurance might have fields for names of drivers and drivers' license numbers. Either a person or an electronic system could compare the field for driver name with the field for driver's license to verify that a driver's license number is provided for each driver's name. That process of comparing fields is called a **cross field check**.

> A **cross field check** is the process of comparing information contained in one data input field with information contained in one or more other fields.

Common types of transaction validation edits include the following:

- Numeric edit: verifies that numbers and not letters are contained in a field

- Alpha edit: verifies that letters and not numbers are contained in a field

- Length edit: verifies that the appropriate number of characters are contained in a field (for example, if drivers' license numbers in a particular state are supposed to have nine characters, only nine-character data will be accepted in that field)

- Range edit: verifies that the data in a field are within prescribed limits (for example, the number of a month must be between 1 and 12)

- List edit: verifies that data in a field match only certain listed possibilities (for example, an auto manufacturer must be one whose name appears on a list)

The requested fields are typically organized to gather data in a specific sequence. The sequence facilitates the system's efficiency in accepting the data. The organization of the requested fields also establishes a uniform data-gathering method that helps ensure that all necessary items are obtained.

Transforming or Processing

The classification process groups the information from source documents into two categories: (1) source documents that satisfy the system's edits and (2) those that require investigation by an underwriter or another person. The system can only process the data from source documents that pass the various edits, so source documents must be complete and accurate. The system processes the data that pass the edits in the following ways:

- *Calculation*—computing premium amounts, bills, adjustments to outstanding balances, commissions, contingent commissions, policyholder dividends, and cancellations

- *Comparison*—determining whether rates match the risk's territory location, whether requested limits are appropriate for the type of policy, whether auto comprehensive coverage is provided if collision is requested, and whether the producer is authorized to write business in the state

- *Summary*—consolidating or aggregating data of similar types to produce meaningful totals, such as total premium written by line of business or within a territory

- *Storage*—recording data for future access in policy files, producer records, commission payments, or claim histories

Some insurers maintain both paper and electronic records of source documents. Insurers with electronic data storage capability can access a wide range of data quickly, providing a record of all transactions for any given policy. Accuracy and completeness of these processed records are essential for determining information about the coverage to which a customer is entitled and the amounts of premium that the insurer can retain for the payment of its losses and expenses and its investment uses. The data that have been processed and recorded provide information that can next be used to generate reports about how the insurer is operating.

Report Generation

Businesses depend on information about their operations to monitor whether they are achieving their expected results. Because insurers pay money for claims when certain information is provided and because insurers are obligated to customers for future payments of money based on certain information, monitoring the accuracy and reliability of that information is crucial. Consequently, the last stage of the processing cycle, report generation, is especially important to insurers.

Exception reports are lists of transactions that fail to pass transaction validation edits. Such failure can occur because the data input is incorrect or because the data do not match the value or description required by the program.

Exception Reports

Because the accuracy of information is crucial, information edits are required to identify transactions that need careful evaluation. **Exception reports** are used to summarize potentially inaccurate transactions or transactions that indicate unusual circumstances. Sometimes transactions fail because of input errors or missing or incorrect data. Exception reports used exclusively to identify errors are often called error reports. Such reports can identify the people responsible for making errors, which is beneficial in defining appropriate remedial training to reduce mistakes.

Exception reports also identify elements of data that do not match predefined selection criteria. For example, underwriting edits for personal auto insurance might be designed to cease processing and refer to underwriters new policy transactions containing a piece of data that indicates drivers under age seventeen. Exception reports can be used to summarize the number of new policies that are referred to underwriters because of such edits.

Another Use for Exception Reports

Exception reports are also an important source of data about the appropriateness of the edits that the system has been instructed to apply. For example, suppose an insurer has experienced a high percentage of claims for hail damage to residence roofs over the past three years. The insurer might begin requiring a data field on all future property insurance applications that specifies the year the roof was last replaced. The insurer might also establish an edit that prevents the system from accepting any residential risk for which the roof has not been replaced in the past ten years. A management exception report might subsequently reveal that the percentage of homeowners applications failing to pass the edit process has increased from 15 percent to 70 percent as a result of the new edit. With 70 percent of the applications failing to pass the edits, the number of applications referred to the underwriters might increase by 500 percent. Such an increase in the number of underwriting referrals could slow processing time and irritate producers and customers, adversely affecting sales.

Management reports that reveal this type of information can bring attention to situations that require action. In this case, the increase in referrals resulting from the edit might mean that the requirement (referral of roofs older than ten years) was unreasonable.

Exception reports are rarely designed to make management decisions. They simply identify the exceptions to some prescribed set of instructions. Analysis of the exception sources typically reveals additional information that can help management in deciding appropriate action.

Production and Processing Reports

Reports that are regularly produced are sometimes called **production reports**, regular production reports, or standard management production reports. They typically show results for a particular time, such as a month, and over a period of time, such as year to date. They are useful for monitoring both current and cumulative results. Processing reports are one type of production report.

> **Production reports** display data in a standardized format and are distributed in paper or electronic form at regular intervals, typically monthly. The term "production" refers to the regular availability and standardized format, not the report content. Consequently, an exception report might be one type of production report. Similarly, processing reports that are distributed routinely according to standardized format are another example of production reports.

A common type of **processing report** is the confirmation report. It lists all transactions (by type and source) that were processed during a specific time period. It confirms the transactions that were processed. Confirmed transactions include records of premiums, claims, and incurred expenses. Another type of processing report is the balancing report, which shows the multiple accounting effects of a single processing transaction. For example, a summary of information about endorsements would show the increases and decreases in premium that resulted from processing various additions and deletions of coverage over some time period. A report showing how written premium was distributed between earned and unearned premium would also be an example of a balancing report.

> **Processing reports** are summaries of data describing actions the system performed. Examples include numbers of applications input, premium recorded, expenses paid, and losses incurred.

Exception and processing reports are sufficiently important to the routine monitoring of insurer results that they are typically produced (on paper or electronically) at least monthly, and sometimes daily. Because many insurer employees and managers regularly need the information contained in these reports, the organization typically standardizes the categories of information and the format in which the information is displayed, which helps report readers quickly locate key items of information for comparison.

Certain production reports summarize the actual results for policy count, endorsement processing, premium, losses, and expenses, and also display the organization's goals or objectives for each of those measures. Many such reports display calculated deviations from the objectives, facilitating results evaluation.

Many insurers provide their management reports on intranet systems, via internal e-mail, or by restricted on-line access to database information. Electronic access permits wide availability of information within an organization and reduces the administrative costs of distribution associated with circulating paper reports.

Special Reports

Although production reports are highly important for routine results and activity monitoring, the information contained in those reports frequently raises questions that require a different level of detail analysis.

> A **special report** is a collection of data selected for a specific purpose and not typically intended for regular distribution. Special reports are sometimes called ad hoc or nonproduction reports.

Special reports, sometimes called ad hoc or nonproduction reports, are usually custom designed by underwriting and portfolio analysis specialists (though once designed, they can be reused to access similar information if needed at a future time). Because of the nature of some insurer systems, the programming expertise of systems specialists is sometimes required to access and sort data for nonproduction reports. Increasingly, however, on-line access to insurer databases is available (to authorized insurer personnel), with user-friendly point-and-click interface technology, from almost anywhere electronic communication is available. Consequently, a skilled portfolio analyst can typically produce detailed analyses of results, on demand, within minutes of perceiving a need for the analysis. That type of information management improves an organization's ability to respond to change, address problems, and take advantage of opportunities before competitors can act. That is why leading insurers have invested heavily in developing effective information management systems.

> ### Example of a Special or Ad Hoc Report
>
> Suppose production reports reveal that an insurer's homeowners premium is increasing by an annual rate of 20 percent and losses are increasing by an annual rate of 25 percent. Production reports are likely to be available at the regional, branch, state, territory, and producer levels. However, understanding whether the types of losses or the causes of increasing premium are similar will require more narrowly defined analysis. An insurer might assemble a data file containing the records of every homeowners policy with a loss in the past three years. A special report might be designed from that data to sort the selected policies by ranges of Coverage A amount, by age of structure, by type of loss, or by any other element of data that was collected and that the insurer's system can retrieve from storage.

Accessing Transaction Information

Since the primary users of insurer information are regulators, stockholders, employees, and management, it is important to consider what types of data are most useful in creating information for those users. Transactions of particular interest to insurer management include the following:

- Underwriting activity that results in premium increases or decreases (new applications, endorsements, and cancellations)
- Premium collections/returns (bill payments and returns of overpayments)
- Loss payments (partial and final claim settlements)
- Expense payments (insurer underwriting and administrative expenses and other overhead)
- Reserve adjustments (loss and unearned premium reserves)

The need for the above transaction information may seem obvious, but to access data to develop useful information requires answering the following questions:

- How are the data recorded?
- Which items of data can be accessed?
- What could data be used for?
- Who can best use the data?
- What happens to the organization when the data are used?

The effectiveness with which an insurer manages information can determine whether it achieves its objectives. Many insurers fail to effectively use the data they have collected. Consider the following telephone conversation between the president (P) and the senior vice president of underwriting (SVP) of hypothetical Galactic Insurance Company on a Friday afternoon in early April.

P: Fred! I can't believe what's happened to our combined ratio this quarter!

What are you doing about it?

SVP: I'm concerned about the increase, too. Remember, I summarized some of the causes in our staff meeting last week.

P: I don't want to hear about the causes right now, Fred. I have a board of directors' meeting next week, and I need some answers about how the results will be improved. Our written premium is 5 percent below our budget. How do we plan to improve the trend in our premium?

SVP: There are several action plans in place to increase the company's premium, but I think we should also be concerned about the growth in our losses.

P: I'm glad you mentioned that. The loss ratio is five points higher than it was a year ago at this time! Five points, Fred! The board of directors will not be pleased. What am I supposed to tell them?

SVP: Well, we've identified the lines of business that are contributing most to the increase in losses, and we're reunderwriting all of the renewals to reduce the high-exposure risks.

P: Fine. And when is that likely to be reflected in the loss ratio, Fred? Next year? Two years from now? We need something immediate. The board expects us to know how to handle exposures before the loss ratio gets out of hand.

SVP: We've filed rate increases in all major states for the unprofitable lines of business. And we've been reducing the scheduled credits on many risks for the past twelve months to improve the loss ratio. We'll know more about how effective those actions have been when our second-quarter results are available for analysis in July.

P: The board won't wait until July. I need you to meet with your senior managers and give me a plan showing how you're going to monitor our results daily from now until whenever we get the premium and losses back on target. I'll need your plan by Monday afternoon at one because the chairman wants to meet with me at five.

Since Galactic has never produced daily reports, Fred is unsure about how to obtain them. He is no more pleased with Galactic's results than the president is, but Fred thinks he is powerless to monitor results on a daily basis. He has become accustomed to assessing results on a monthly basis because many of Galactic's production reports are summarized and distributed monthly, even though the data are gathered as every transaction is input.

Fred has worked at Galactic for over thirty years, and he recalls that, when he worked as a commercial fire underwriter, he read, evaluated, and rated every application for coverage. He kept a daily log of new applications submitted by each agent, which included the premium and coverage amounts and the accumulated total of premium written by each agent. He also reviewed each loss report prepared for the policies he accepted and recorded payments and reserves in the same manual log along with the premium. He could check the current year-to-date results for any of his agents just by reading his log. Using his manual information system, he could monitor results on a daily basis.

Fred began to wonder how he could do the same using an electronic information system. He phoned the vice presidents of marketing, claims, administration, and information systems to set up a meeting. On Monday at 1:00 P.M., he met with the President.

P: I was really pleased to hear your optimism about daily results monitoring when you phoned me at home Saturday night. I have to admit that I was *not* encouraged by your reaction to that idea when we talked on Friday afternoon.

SVP: I began to think about how I used to monitor results before I became accustomed to assessing our performance from monthly system production reports. I could assess results daily from manual reports. Our system records a very high level of detail on every transaction, more than I could ever have recorded as an underwriter, but it seemed that the volume of detail was preventing us from accessing it any time other than monthly. Our month-end production reports are a compilation of many sources of data that are cross-checked for accuracy, and, because they're so useful, we've begun to depend on them as our only source of key information.

P: It sounds like you had our systems people involved.

SVP: Yes, Barbara's been a great addition as our new officer of information technology. Much of the plan was possible because of her understanding of how to access data. Jim was also a great help with his creative approach to problem analysis. I guess that's why he's such a good marketing manager. But everyone contributed to our proposal. Cathy's years of experience with our administrative processes and work flow analysis helped us to reexamine our work flow. Paul's understanding of the claim records was also important in designing the proposal.

P: So give me a quick overview of your plan for daily information monitoring.

SVP: We've actually taken the concept a step further. We decided that it wasn't enough to monitor information from different systems. What we really wanted was the ability to manage our results as they were developing. For example, I wanted to be aware of any exceptions our underwriters were making as they were making them. Paul wanted to be informed of preliminary loss reports on any losses with estimated reserves over $25,000 as soon as the reports were received.

P: Weren't you concerned that being overly involved in that level of detail might slow our processing ability?

SVP: Yes. Cathy and Jim reminded us that if we interrupted the flow of work among underwriters or claim representatives, we could slow down service so much that we could delay claim processing and customer service, and that would hurt our flow of business. Plus, our employees might think we've lost confidence in them and have started to micromanage the operation. Our goal was to manage information as it becomes available, not disrupt our existing work processes.

P: What exactly do you mean by "managing information as it becomes available"?

SVP: We spent a lot of time defining that. Daily monitoring could get us a faster assessment of our results, but by itself it wouldn't improve results. We wanted to have a better understanding of our daily activity so that we could adjust our underwriting, pricing, and service guidelines quickly if we needed to. Those adjustments have the potential of changing results. For example, we wanted to be able to identify why the percentage of rejected new business quotes is higher for some underwriters than others, and we didn't want to wait until the end of the month to observe changes. We had information about prior-year successful quote figures by month and by underwriter. It was easy to develop an average for each underwriter and for the company as a whole.

P: But you wouldn't expect all underwriters to have the same ratio, would you?

SVP: No, because some underwriters work with producers in highly competitive environments where it's always going to be more difficult to close the sale. So we reviewed a sampling of quotes sent by every underwriter over the past month and assessed the reasonableness of their practices to establish an approximate deviation from average for each underwriter. With that we could identify quote rates by underwriter and closely evaluate the decisions of underwriters with quote rates that deviate from the average.

P: If you ask the underwriters to review quotes just because their success rate is different from the average, won't that interfere with the work flow?

SVP: We won't ask the underwriters to conduct the review. We'll be asking the front-line supervisors and managers to perform the review of deviations, and they'll have to evaluate the causes of the deviations. We suspect most of the deviations will be justifiable, but some may pinpoint problems that we in management have unintentionally created by defining possibly inappropriate guidelines for certain producers or conditions.

P: Won't all this checking require a lot of manual work for our supervisors?

SVP: That's where our information system saves us. Although we've used the system's ability to calculate successful quote percentages on a monthly basis, we haven't used its ability to calculate daily percentages by underwriter. We created a test inquiry format over the weekend that compares each underwriter's daily results with his or her prior-month and year-to-date average. So the system can do the checking and let the supervisor know when a significant deviation occurs.

P: Won't the underwriters feel like we're watching them too closely?

SVP: You're right; that could be a problem. They might feel as though they're being punished for something. But we don't think so, and here's why.

Fred explained that he would try to enlist the underwriters' help in using the statistics to identify problems with Galactic's pricing or underwriting guidelines.

P: So you plan to manage our information by giving more of it to our underwriters and asking them to manage it?

SVP: Well, yes...and we aren't planning to stop with the underwriters.

P: Tell me more.

Fred said that he wanted to record the average length of time that elapsed between loss notification and the claim department's first contact with the insured or claimant. He also mentioned several businesses that improved their profit and growth dramatically when strong performers were recognized and rewarded for achieving superior results. Turnover, he cautioned, would probably rise as a result of the employee-level information monitoring. Nevertheless, the president was pleased with the proposal.

Now consider whether Galactic's president obtained answers to the questions that began this section.

How are the data recorded? He learned that transactions are recorded individually as they occur. That means transactions can be summarized daily or otherwise, if desired. If the system allows real-time access, transactions can be counted and summarized on demand. Many systems currently allow on-demand access to transaction information.

Which items of data can be accessed? Although he does not know all of the possible transactions that could be accessed, he knows that data about under-writing and claim activities can be accessed and that the information has potential value.

What could the data be used for? Fred has identified data that provide information about successful quote ratios and claim handling. Many other uses seem possible.

Who can best use the data? Underwriters, producers, administrators, claim representatives, and members of management will find value in this informa-tion for benchmarking average performance, comparing their own perfor-mance to benchmarks and past averages, and assessing changes in their performance.

What happens to the organization when the data are used? The insurer becomes more aware of its performance at all levels of the organization. That awareness means that outstanding performers can be better recognized as marginal performers become apparent. Although that awareness should help the orga-nization improve its overall achievement of objectives, it is likely to displease some employees who prefer not to change. Consequently, some increased turnover is likely as information is more effectively managed.

Needs for Information

Insurers require information to do the following:

- Monitor results for premium, losses, and expenses
- Meet requirements of statistical reporting organizations
- Maximize processing capabilities
- Evaluate and improve work flow
- Assess customer satisfaction
- Gather employee input
- Audit procedural and regulatory compliance

Although insurers have other information needs, this text limits discussion to the seven identified above.

Computer systems play an important role in collecting data, classifying data, converting data to information, and reporting. Although an insurer could use separate computer systems to collect and store data to meet its different information needs, most insurers limit their number of computer systems to three or fewer. One computer system might be used to evaluate and process new policies, produce statistical and processing reports, monitor administra-tive processes and employee performance, and perform underwriting and processing audits. A separate computer system might be used to record claim data and monitor claim processing and paid losses. A manual system might be used to assess customer satisfaction. However, insurer needs are the same whether information is accessed electronically, by one or more systems, or manually.

Monitor Results

Organizations have an abundance of data available collected for a range of specific purposes. As discussed earlier in this chapter, state regulators represent one significant group of data users. Insurers collect and classify a high level of detailed data that are routinely sent to regulatory authorities. However, because the data are not needed for most routine information purposes, that level of detail is not typically used for production reports. Consequently, many insurer employees who might be able to use more detailed data to better understand their business responsibilities are not aware that the detail exists. Even those who are aware of it may not know how to access the data or how they might use the data to get meaningful information.

A typical month-end production report used to inform marketing and underwriting management might look like the excerpt in Exhibit 1-2.

Exhibit 1-2
Excerpt From Monthly Production Report

| | | Written Premium | | | | |
| | | June | | | YTD | |
	actual	plan	deviation	actual	plan	deviation
MLOB*						
PAL	600	660	− 9.1%	3,800	3,960	− 4.0%
PAPD	420	480	− 12.5%	2,460	2,880	− 14.6%
F	200	200	0	1,300	1,200	+ 8.3%
H	1,010	950	+ 6.3%	6,050	6,000	+ 0.8%
CGL	400	380	+ 5.3%	2,200	2,200	0
WC	500	500	0	2,800	3,000	− 6.7%
CAL	800	750	+ 6.7%	4,350	4,500	− 3.3%
CAPD	300	280	+ 7.1%	2,000	1,600	+ 25.0%
TOTAL	4,230	4,200	+ 0.7%	24,960	25,340	− 1.5%

*Major Line of Business: personal auto liability (PAL), personal auto physical damage (PAPD), fire (F), homeowners (H), commercial general liability (CGL), workers compensation (WC), commercial auto liability (CAL), and commercial auto physical damage (CAPD).

Exhibit 1-2 shows only written premium. Most production reports also provide major headings for earned premium, expenses, expense ratio, paid and incurred losses, loss ratio, loss frequency, and loss severity. Some reports also show premium and losses for one or more prior years at the same time and/or year to date. Some calculate percentage changes from the previous month for each major heading. Other reports include counts, by major line, of new business, endorsements, and renewals processed. The content of production reports is limited only by the needs of the primary users. Insurers with different functional departments (such as underwriting, marketing, claims, and administration) commonly generate multiple versions of the monthly production reports to satisfy the particular needs of each functional area.

Consequently, the claim department monthly report might emphasize the number of new claims received, the number of reserve adjustments made, changes in the average value of new reserves, average times to close files, average length of time to first claimant contact, changes in numbers of claims pending, and differences in frequency and severity by major line. The underwriting department might be particularly interested in monitoring quote acceptance ratios, exceptions to underwriting guidelines, and loss ratios.

Experienced insurance professionals often request and review copies of the monthly production reports used by other functional departments. Claim representatives can discover useful information among data that are regularly distributed to underwriters but not to claim personnel. Underwriters might find value in reviewing reports routinely used by administrators to summarize average processing time in each department. Different combinations of information displayed on production reports tend to evolve to meet the most common data needs of each functional area; however, changing needs are not typically reflected in the design and content of the production report. Periodic reexamination of production report design is beneficial for identifying possible alternate content. It also serves an important purpose of reminding report users that additional data are available not only for possible inclusion in production reports, but also for analyses that might benefit from the generation of ad hoc reports.

One of the purposes of this chapter is to consider how different types of data can best be used to better understand a particular business. Data can be sorted and organized in infinitely different ways. The range of possibilities intimidates even the most experienced and technologically competent managers. Insurers select and sort data in different combinations to develop information to better understand their organizations. Managers typically demand access to certain types of information that they believe will be most helpful in their routine responsibilities. They specify which sources of data they want summarized and how they want the summary organized, or formatted, for printed reports or on a computer screen. Once management has defined specific data needs, production reports summarizing the data in an established format are usually distributed on a regular basis (weekly or monthly). One common production report used by insurers, sometimes called a premium production report, summarizes data for written premium, earned premium, incurred losses, and underwriting expenses for each major line of business.

Summaries of data typically combine, or aggregate, detailed levels of data into various summary levels. For example, the highest level of a production report for written premium for Large Insurance Company (LIC) might combine all of the company's policy premiums. Another level of the production report might combine policy data by state, and another level might summarize by producer. Those combinations of aggregated data help those who use the reports to interpret data and to extract useful information from the reports.

Production reports provide data that reflect actual business results. Insurers compare production report data with the expected values for each result category measured. Insurers typically establish premium objectives. If, for example, Insurer T establishes a monthly written premium goal of $2 million, and the production report shows premium to be $1.9 million, insurer management can readily know that actual premium is less than expected. The difference between the actual values that appear in the production report and the expected values is sometimes called a deviation or a variance. Multiple levels of production reports can be used to pinpoint the major locations of deviations, but insurers typically use special or ad hoc reports to investigate specific causes of deviations. In the example of Insurer T, management might examine production reports by geographic region or producer to locate those with the greatest deviations from expected values. However, management might use special reports to identify trends in premium growth for those regions or producers to better understand the deviation. Consequently, both production and special reports are crucial for the management of insurer information.

Meet Statistical Reporting Requirements

Insurers report a great deal of data to the National Association of Insurance Commissioners (NAIC) and to statistical data collection organizations like ISO. Most of the data reported to the NAIC is presented in insurer annual financial statements. Although a detailed analysis of insurer annual financial statements is beyond the scope of this text, it is helpful to be aware of the detail available from that source. Selected information from the insurer annual financial statements is reproduced or condensed in the annual reports (which detail an insurer's operating results) to stockholders and policyholders.

Raw data needed to produce the annual financial statements and the annual reports are usually retained in either paper or electronic form. Consequently, if an insurer employee or manager needs to access information in annual statements and reports, it is available for the creation of ad hoc reports.

For example, LIC has been experiencing deteriorating loss ratios on its private passenger auto business. The marketing manager recently had his car stolen and knows LIC pays for many stolen vehicles, so he might suspect the loss ratio problem concerns increasing incidence of theft. The underwriting manager has seen several recent underwriting files that revealed the failure of customers to disclose property damage losses under $500. She thinks the problem might be caused by increased property damage claims and the failure of customers to disclose their past property damage losses. The claim manager has experienced recent problems with two large uninsured motorists losses, and he thinks that the loss ratio deterioration might be from that coverage. Each insurance professional brings a different set of experiences to the interpretation of results. That experience can be helpful in interpreting results and in considering possible action, but it can also lead to conclusions that the facts do not substantiate. Production reports might distinguish between private passenger auto liability and physical damage premium and losses, but those reports do not usually provide a more detailed breakdown of the experience.

NAIC reporting requires that insurers collect and classify substantially detailed data according to what is sometimes called major and minor lines. The distinction between major and minor lines illustrates how users of data can assemble different views of the types of coverage. **Major lines** were shown in Exhibit 1-2 and include such coverages as personal auto liability and personal auto physical damage. If an insurer wishes to know its auto liability loss ratio and its auto physical damage loss ratio, analysis of major line data is appropriate. When detailed results for minor lines of business are desired, the premium and loss data are classified for each component, or subclassification, of the major line. For example, the components of the major line private passenger auto liability usually include bodily injury liability, property damage liability, personal injury protection (if any), medical payments, and uninsured/underinsured motorists coverage. Those components, or subclassifications, of the major line are called **minor lines**.

> **Major lines** include personal auto liability, personal auto physical damage, and workers compensation. **Minor lines** are subclassifications of the major lines. Examples of minor lines for the major line of personal auto liability are bodily injury liability, property damage liability, and uninsured motorists coverage.

Because data are collected and classified by minor lines, the data can be used to produce ad hoc reports that describe premium and loss experience for each of those minor lines. A study of the premium and loss experience by minor line might reveal that all of LIC's managers, in the above example, are incorrect in their guesses about the source of the deteriorating loss ratio. Detailed results analysis could reveal that the deterioration is caused by higher-than-normal bodily injury liability losses or by some other component of coverage.

How Much Detail?

Effective information management requires that data be examined at the appropriate level of detail. If the detail is available, analysis can reveal significant information to aid decision making. In this case, if LIC discovered that its unsatisfactory loss experience was caused by some aspect of its private passenger auto bodily injury coverage, such as an increase in the average severity of bodily injury losses, it might decide to file appropriately higher rates for bodily injury liability, while leaving rates for other minor lines unchanged. Similarly, if an analysis of other minor lines revealed that experience was better than expected, LIC might decide to lower rates for those other coverages. Decreases in rates for other coverages might offset part of a bodily injury coverage rate increase and minimize negative customer reaction to higher overall policy premiums.

Detailed statistical data collected for the needs of the NAIC and advisory or statistical organizations might also provide insight about insurer results. For example, statistical organizations often require insurers to submit detailed data about their rating variables and classifications. Insurers therefore collect and classify data by rate class, geographic territory, pricing tier or track (if multiple tiers or tracks are used), coverage limit, and many other rating variables. So insurers can often develop an ad hoc report that shows at least premium and losses by those rating variables.

LIC might further specify the cause of its auto bodily injury liability loss ratio. It might find, for example, that the loss ratio is highest in certain territories, among pleasure-rated vehicles, that have minimum limits of liability. That information might suggest distributing a rate increase disproportionately among the rating classes so that the classes with the greatest losses experience an appropriately greater portion of the rate increase.

Information gained from this sort of ad hoc report might also suggest a need to conduct a special underwriting review of all policies that have certain rating characteristics. Most information systems can identify all policies that meet specified characteristics, or parameters, in a matter of minutes. Portfolio analysts and underwriters can then review policies identified by the system as possessing the defined characteristics to determine similarities that might reveal the possible causes of unusual loss experience. If causes can be isolated by such analysis, LIC might decide to adjust rates for a narrower range of risks or to restrict underwriting acceptability to a narrowly defined group of policyholders.

Production reports, whether printed or electronic, are important tools for monitoring major categories of insurer performance, including total written premium, earned premium, incurred losses, and underwriting expenses. However, because production reports are used so frequently, insurance professionals often begin to assume that available data are limited to the categories displayed in the production reports. Ad hoc reports provide access to greater detail so that analysts can better understand the factors influencing results. The data collected, classified, and sorted for use by the NAIC and other statistical collection organizations are an important source of detailed information.

Maximize Administrative Processing Capabilities

Insurers achieve greatest efficiency when their administrative processes are managed effectively. Administrative processes include review and referral of insurance applications and endorsement requests, recording of premium payments and transactions, generation of bills, and preparation of cancellation notices and policy documents. An administrative processing system that performs these functions might also be used to perform all or part of the statistical reporting functions discussed above.

Processing new applications, endorsements to existing policies, and claims continues to be an important component of insurer work flow. Manual processing is still necessary for many functions, but many electronic systems now include decision-making computer programs (called logic protocols) that permit the system to differentiate among many transaction details. For example, many administrative processing systems scan applications with laser optics to streamline the data entry process. Some systems can evaluate collected data for completeness, pursue missing information electronically, distinguish among levels of underwriting expertise needed to evaluate referrals, transfer information to appropriate levels of authority, and issue policies for risks that satisfy minimum requirements.

Administrative processing systems now handle a large portion of the once manual work flow for many insurers. However, the advantages offered by such systems go beyond improving efficiency of insurer operations. Many systems, especially those using electronic data sources, have untapped capabilities. For example, the hypothetical Clever and Wise Insurers (CWI) installed an administrative processing system primarily to screen, rate, and issue its businessowners policies (BOP) ten years ago. As CWI began to understand the capability of its system, it learned that the system could accept applications electronically from producers and directly from customers. It could also electronically compare the fields contained in the application for matches with defined underwriting and pricing guidelines, referring to underwriters any risks that exceed acceptable limits defined by the guidelines. In addition, it could record deposit premiums, initiate commission payments to producers, establish a billing sequence, print a declarations page and policy jacket, and forward both statistical and financial data to other reporting systems maintained by CWI. It could also generate electronic daily management reports to show how many policies are written, the premium amounts, the distribution by customer Standard Industrial Classification (SIC) codes (which are categories of business type, such as manufacturer and service provider), geographic territory, and state. The system now effectively handles 85 percent of the new policies that CWI issues.

Administrative Processing Systems: Tapping Hidden Potential

Many insurers would be pleased with the capability that CWI receives from its administrative processing system, particularly if they were receiving investment income of 10 percent in addition to 12 points of underwriting profit. However, CWI managers were not satisfied. They noticed that the system had further untapped capabilities. Because it collected detailed data describing coverage amounts, customer SIC codes, specific ZIP Code geographic locations, and all of the rating variables used in pricing the businessowners policy, CWI management began wondering how the data might help them better determine which customers should be charged less and which should be charged more based on CWI's loss experience.

They accessed policy information from their administrative processing system, claim data from their claim processing system, and premium and loss history from their statistical reporting database. Next, they sorted the data for the five most common rating classifications. By merging premium and claim statistical information with the processing system, CWI managers designed a program that permitted the processing system to assign a range of premium credits and debits to reflect the most recent thirty-six months of premium and claim experience. (By using premium and loss experience over three years, they minimized the effects of large losses and short-term changes in results.) The result was an ability to use the most recent three years of data from multiple sources to adjust the administrative processing system's application of rate credits and debits (surcharges) according to the relative differences in loss experience over time.

In states where CWI obtained regulator approval for the use of this flexible system, it reduced rates among customers in SIC code classes with favorable loss experience. Therefore, CWI offered a lower price than many of its competitors. By adjusting its debit and credit structure monthly (within a prescribed range filed with the state) according to its evolving experience, CWI improved the responsiveness of its rates sufficiently to reduce the loss ratio three points over the next three years while growing aggressively.

CWI managers still were not satisfied. They noted that their system could issue 85 percent of the applications received without referral to underwriters. Issued policies were immediately recorded in the system so that if a claim occurred, claim representatives could immediately make coverage determinations. They discovered that a customer could apply for coverage electronically at 9:00 A.M. using e-mail, fax, or Internet home page communication. If the system approved the application, the customer could receive verification of policy issuance by 9:30 A.M. If desired, coverage confirmation could be provided electronically as soon as the customer paid the premium. If a customer made the deposit premium payment with a credit card or other electronic funds transfer method, coverage could be verified as soon as the system evaluated and accepted the application data.

CWI management decided to market the administrative processing system's capability to rapidly evaluate electronically submitted applications. A sales strategy was developed using e-mail listings of businesses in the three most profitable SIC code classes. Electronic premium quotes were solicited. As CWI's system rated the application data to generate the quote, it simultaneously evaluated the risk characteristics for acceptability and offered to bind coverage with a valid credit card payment. For customers who were pleased with the quote but preferred to wait until their existing coverage expired to change to CWI, the system confirmed the quote electronically and mailed a hard copy confirmation to the future customer. The system sent a bill for coverage sixty days before the desired effective date. This sales strategy increased CWI's total written premium by 30 percent over the first two years. CWI management was particularly pleased with the new-found uses of data, particularly since they already had the system and it cost very little to expand its ability.

> **Data warehousing** is the process of storing data for the purpose of using it later. **Data mining** is the process of accessing warehoused data.

CWI is a hypothetical company, but it serves as an example of the potential uses administrative processing systems can provide, such as **data warehousing** and **data mining**. Since mining warehoused data can improve an insurer's understanding of its results, problems, and opportunities (often for little additional cost), those responsible for insurer performance are increasingly exploring expanded uses of available data for the valuable information they can produce.

Evaluate and Improve Work Flow

All organizations need information with which to monitor organizational performance. Insurers are primarily interested in monitoring premium, losses, and expenses. Production reports provide essential data in these categories, and ad hoc reports can identify additional data with which to understand deviations from expected results. However, insurers also need to evaluate how well administrative processing functions are being performed, and most production reports are limited in how well they address this need.

Insurers are service organizations that meet customer needs by collecting and processing data to create information. Insurance customers need to transfer risk of potential loss and are willing to pay to accomplish that. For the insurance transaction to occur, a customer must make representations on an application, agree to abide by the conditions of the policy, and pay a premium. In return, the insurer establishes a detailed record of the agreement to transfer risk, which is then documented to the customer with a policy. Electronic records of the insurance transaction provide evidence of the insurance transaction so that coverage can be verified for insureds, lienholders, mortgagees, regulators, and claimants. For the insurance transaction to occur, several administrative procedures must occur. Following are some typical stages of administrative processing:

1. Application received (electronically or on paper)
2. Application checked for completeness, risk acceptability, and pricing
3. Deposit premium, if any, recorded and deposited
4. Application data fields input to a computer system
5. Data classified and application referred or policy issued
6. Policy documents produced
7. Premium billing record established

8. Policyholder record established
9. Commissions paid to producers
10. Statistical and financial records produced

An insurer's administrative processing system performs many of the tasks mentioned above. For example, a typical insurer might sell personal auto liability and physical damage, homeowners, businessowners, commercial auto liability and physical damage, workers compensation, and general liability coverages. Most insurer systems count the number of applications received daily for each of those major lines of business. The system probably also counts the number of correspondence items (whether received on paper or electronically) that the insurer receives daily. Correspondences might include requests from customers to change or endorse coverage on an existing policy, notice of a claim, or an inquiry for information.

In addition, insurers anticipate that most of their customers will choose to renew their policies after any particular policy period expires. For that reason, they typically evaluate the accumulated information for each customer as if the customer had requested an additional period of coverage. Customers that continue to satisfy the insurer's underwriting guidelines are usually offered a renewal of coverage. Most insurers process at least applications for coverage, requests for changes and endorsements, and renewals.

An insurer's work in process includes applications not yet reviewed, items of correspondence (requests for changes, endorsements, cancellations, and claim reports), and renewal policies. For example, in a given week, an insurer might receive 200 applications, 400 items of correspondence, and 600 renewals that require underwriting, rating, and other processing. Insurer inventories are usually made up of incomplete service work, which is similar to a manufacturer's work in process. Exhibit 1-3 illustrates how a work in process summary might look for an insurer.

Exhibit 1-3
Insurer Work in Process Summary

Category of Work	# at start of week	# received during week	# left over at end of wk	# processed during week
Applications	25	200	15	210
Correspondence	21	400	6	415
Renewals	36	600	50	586

Exhibit 1-3 reveals that the insurer had fewer applications and items of correspondence left over at the end of the week than it had at the beginning of the week. It also reveals that the insurer had more renewals on hand at the end of the week than at the beginning of the week. If insurer management monitor categories of work in a manner similar to Exhibit 1-3, over time they will notice changes in the number of items received and processed each week.

Few insurers receive a perfectly consistent flow of applications, correspondence, and renewals each week. Similarly, few insurers have so consistent a supply of employees that the volume of work handled each week would be the same. Temporary reassignments of people, illnesses, and vacations affect an insurer's ability to deliver the same level of productivity each week. However, a monitoring tool, such as a work in process monitoring system, can help to identify the average amounts of each type of work that is processed each week and to establish an average of how much of each type of work the organization receives and processes.

Monitoring Systems: Tapping Hidden Potential

Monitoring systems can be helpful in other ways. An insurer might wish to understand how applications, correspondences, and renewals vary among different major lines of business. It could establish a monitoring system that counts applications, correspondences, and renewals by line of business. Doing so would help identify trends in the mix of new business, the differences in correspondence activity, and seasonal variations in renewals by line of business.

Monitoring systems might also include additional categories of work. For example, a personal lines direct writing insurer might want to monitor telephone activity. Such a company might monitor the number and length of calls by line of business, by geographic territory, or by telephone customer service representative.

Some insurers have found such monitoring helpful in learning how much time it takes on average to perform specific tasks. If an insurer discovers that the average underwriter needs ten minutes to handle an application for personal auto insurance, it might use that average as a standard against which new employees are measured. Training might be implemented to help new employees to reach the ten-minute standard. Employees who handle applications more rapidly than the standard would be identifiable so that appropriate audits of their underwriting thoroughness could be conducted. Employees who can meet thoroughness standards but who work more rapidly could be rewarded for their higher levels of productivity.

Another advantage such monitoring offers management is an assessment of needed resources. For example, after several months of measuring administrative processes, such as number of applications received and reviewed, an insurer can determine the current average number of applications that each underwriter handles. The measurements might show that one underwriter can handle the processing responsibilities for 2,500 policies that generate $2 million in premium. That information could be useful in planning the number of employees needed when the insurer anticipates a change in its number of policies. Similarly, if an insurer anticipates several employees being on vacation for a specified time period, understanding how many employees are needed to handle anticipated work facilitates planning to maintain desired levels of service. For example, an insurer might use information from process monitoring to assign overtime responsibility to nonvacationing employees or to make temporary alternative processing arrangements by redistributing work.

Assess Customer Satisfaction

Besides using data from process monitoring systems, many insurers collect data from their customers. Such data can be used to develop information to assess the following:

- Identify key customers
- Customers' perceptions of the insurer's products and services
- Interaction with customers by insurer personnel

Identify Customers

The customer-centered focus of management that began in the late 1980s has had a dramatic effect on how insurers deliver services. In short, insurers discovered that their customers must be their primary concern when they make any business decision.

Insurers assess the satisfaction of their customers in many different ways. Surveys and focus groups provide data about customer perceptions. Telephone monitoring of customer service contacts helps assess appropriateness of employee courtesy. The percentage of existing customers retained for consecutive years is another important type of data used to assess customer satisfaction. State insurance department complaints per million dollars of written premium are yet another measure of customer satisfaction.

Insurers that market through independent agents and brokers typically recognize their producers as an additional group of important customers. Producers seek insurers who are reliable, who provide quality claim service and accurate billing and record keeping, and who offer quality products that policyholders value. Producers also like insurers that are easy to work with.

Customer Perceptions

Most insurers choose products and define rates and underwriting guidelines to attract a particular group of customers. That is an essential component of product planning and pricing. However, most insurers are less effective at collecting data that help monitor customer perceptions over time. Frequently, insurers assume their services are meeting customer expectations until some unexpected negative results occur, such as declining sales or an increasing frequency of customer complaints

A better way to monitor customers' perceptions is to ask them. One insurer decided to collect customer data by performing an annual customer satisfaction survey. Another formed a producer advisory council that meets four times a year to obtain input about how well underwriters, claim representatives, and loss control personnel are meeting customer expectations. Some insurers establish focus group meetings with representatives of key customer groups to assess developing coverage and service needs. One company sends a letter to all claimants with its final claim settlement checks inviting criticism and praise for the personnel involved in the handling of the loss. Many insurers with large customer service operations routinely monitor employee–customer telephone interaction to evaluate the level of courtesy provided by employees.

However insurers choose to collect customer data, they must classify the data according to how the data will best benefit insurer objectives. Assessing the degree to which current customer expectations are being met can help the organization affirm that it is performing as well as it wants to perform. When customers express satisfaction, additional marketing opportunities might be identified. Emerging customer needs can motivate the modification or creation of products, frequently generating additional sales.

Whether customer perceptions are based on correct or incorrect interpretations of fact, insurers can better manage their products and operations by improving their understanding of what customers believe. The perception is frequently more important than the reality. An insurer that has consistently provided prompt and fair claim settlement to hundreds of customers might receive negative publicity for two or three claims handled poorly during a major catastrophe. Assessing customer perceptions and publicizing favorable impressions can counter negative publicity. Insurers that successfully monitor and respond to customer needs will be better able to influence the development of customer perceptions.

Interaction of Customers and Insurer Personnel

Demands by insurance consumers for uniformly high quality claim service have resulted in most insurers' carefully monitoring the interaction of claim personnel with policyholders and claimants. Among data customarily recorded in the claim handling process are the elapsed time between first notice of loss (from the customer or claimant to the insurer) and first contact (by the insurer) with the customer or claimant, and the time between that contact and the loss settlement date. Measurement of these times has become more common as a result of insurer needs to prove prompt and efficient claim handling. Because of its access to detailed data that measure the timing of its operations (including interaction with customers), one insurer established an objective to make first contact after notice of a claim within twenty minutes. Whereas most insurers might be content to make first contact within twenty-four hours, this insurer's objective set an ambitious goal for employees that elevated employee awareness of the importance of prompt customer service and dramatically improved the company's reputation for being customer focused. Although twenty minutes can be an impossible goal for customer contact in many claim situations, by establishing that objective, the insurer used customer interaction data as a tool to improve its product, elevate its image among customers, and distinguish itself from competitors.

Monitoring insurer–customer interaction is also common in managing customer service operations. Besides periodic monitoring of conversations between employees and customers, many customer service departments solicit comments and suggestions from their customers. Although some customers refuse to respond to service surveys, others not only complete short survey forms but also offer letters of thanks for service they perceive to be unusually good. Insurers that receive such comments often circulate or publish them within their organization as evidence of the quality they can deliver. Visibility given to exceptional employee performance can motivate similar behavior among other employees, particularly if it is routinely monitored and recognized.

Interaction between insurer personnel and insurance producers is another crucial process to be monitored. For example, producers develop expectations that underwriters will provide expertise, professionalism, and prompt, courteous service. Insurers that develop an ability to meet those needs will encourage inquiries for new business quotes and improve retention of existing accounts. Insurer management must be attentive to producer perceptions of whether insurer personnel are meeting those expectations. Surveys and focus groups might not be practical methods for assessing producer perceptions of underwriters' (or other professional staff members') performance. However, meetings between producers and underwriting (or marketing) management occur frequently enough for insurers to collect information about the strengths and weaknesses of technical staff members. Such input requires careful interpretation and evaluation.

Regulators, external suppliers, and other insurer divisions, although not typically perceived as customers, are important to an insurer's effective operation. Establishing appropriate policies for quality service to these customers is equally important to the insurer's success. Some insurers assign the responsibility for regulator contact to a limited number of individuals in an effort to guarantee a level of consistency in communication quality. Others require written summaries of regulator interaction to be filed with specified corporate relations specialists.

Regulators are not the only external customers with whom insurer personnel interact. Since insurers often depend on outside services for such items as risk inspections, loss control and audit reports, claim investigations, and legal consultations, collecting data about those interactions permits monitoring the effectiveness of those service providers. Service providers who know that their products are being continuously evaluated tend to pay attention to their customers' expectations. Insurers seeking to establish a reputation for high-quality, prompt, and courteous service tend to demand the same kind of service from their suppliers. Management must monitor how well those relationships support the insurer's overall objectives.

Interactions with internal customers should also be monitored. Different departments or divisions of organizations frequently provide services to each other. Although many organizations deliver high levels of customer service among their various departments and divisions, internal suppliers might become complacent. If they believe their internal customers have no choice but to use their service, they might be less concerned about the quality they deliver. They might believe they have a monopoly on the type of service they provide. To verify that such complacency is not weakening the quality of service received by internal customers, many insurers collect data about service time in different departments and perform operational procedure audits to assess the reasonableness of established work flows.

Operational Procedure Auditing: A Case Study

The underwriting department of the hypothetical Reliable Insurance Company (RIC) depends on a separate loss control engineering department for information necessary to evaluate the pricing of commercial property risks. If the loss control department cannot provide adequate detail in their reports, or if the loss control department is inadequately staffed to meet the demand, the underwriting decision process could be slowed. That reduction in service could be reflected in RIC's losing business or inadequately pricing risks. However, collecting data about the thoroughness of reports and service time informs RIC's management of when service from departments, like loss control in this example, fails to meet internal customer needs.

Some insurers permit internal departments to purchase services from independent outside sources if costs are equal or less and service is better. Such insurers place their internal service providers in direct competition with similar providers outside of the organization. In the early 1990s, one large international insurer that monitored the time services and interdepartmental costs associated with its data processing department chose to outsource a large portion of its systems work because foreign providers demonstrated the ability to meet high standards at substantially lower cost than internal providers. Such measures help ensure that internal departments are attentive to the needs of their internal customers and manage their operations to achieve efficiency and quality as if they were independent businesses.

Gather Employee Input

Insurers use data about the quality and timeliness of work flow and interdepartmental services to establish standards and to measure how organizational objectives are met. However, insurers can also benefit from obtaining input from employees about how they perceive the organization's effectiveness. Some insurers depend on voluntary employee input through such passive devices as suggestion boxes and attendance at group meetings with members of management. Other insurers establish networks of employees who regularly communicate about work issues with which they have direct involvement. Such networks are asked to identify problems and opportunities independently and to define and initiate appropriate action with minimal management involvement.

Employee Input: A Case Study

One insurer assigns groups of managers at different levels of different product divisions to meet quarterly to discuss each other's results. This cross-functional group reviews data measuring written premium, service quality, administrative processing, and claim handling from each of the represented divisions. Each manager is expected to offer recommendations for improving the organization's overall performance. Recommendations may relate to only the divisions represented at the meeting or to others. A summary of the recommendations is shared among attending managers, managers of any of the affected functional areas or divisions, and the level of management above each attendee. Subsequent meetings review changes in performance that result from suggestions developed in the group meetings. The annual performance evaluation of each attendee includes a review of how effectively the individual contributed to achieving group objectives.

Many other approaches to soliciting employee input exceed the scope of this chapter. However, the increasing need for insurers to respond rapidly to changing competition suggests that the hierarchical process characteristic of many traditional organizations may slow the employee input process. Employee feedback, actively solicited, can provide insurer management with meaningful data about day-to-day operations and customer satisfaction. Information developed from such data can help management make business decisions. In addition, employees who see evidence that the organization values their input can gain a greater sense of participation in achieving the organization's results.

Employees who are given accurate data about their performance and who are shown how their performance compares with performance benchmarks have a better understanding of what the organization expects of them. Use of employee input permits the insurer to learn from its employees and to assess possible strengths and weaknesses that were previously less well understood.

Audit Procedural and Regulatory Compliance

An audit is a comparison of specific results with a set of standards. Audits are used in the insurance business to evaluate financial results, verify that producers are adhering to underwriting and accounting guidelines, determine whether personnel are following underwriting, procedural, and pricing practices, demonstrate compliance with regulatory requirements, and ensure use of efficient work flow. Besides the comparison of actual results with expected results, audit data help to compare results over time.

Financial Audits

Data from insurer financial audits help answer the following questions:

- Are existing investments appropriate for the insurer's needs?
- Are investments reasonably conservative?

- Can investments be converted to cash if they are needed to pay for losses?
- Are the values assigned to investments realistic?
- Are the estimates of premiums due reasonable?
- Are the assessments of accounts receivable realistic?
- Are claim reserves (for known losses and for incurred-but-not-reported losses) reasonable?
- Do expenses exceed by a significant amount the insurer's current financial obligations?

Financial audits of insurers are conducted by the insurer's accounting staff, by independent Certified Public Accountants (CPAs), and by representatives of regulatory authorities like the state insurance departments and the federal Securities and Exchange Commission (SEC).

Besides verifying the reasonableness of the insurer's measure of assets, liabilities, and policyholders' surplus, financial audits determine the appropriateness of the insurer's financial controls. Evaluating controls could include determining how effectively the insurer collects premium due from producers or customers. Collection procedures must be implemented for customers and producers who fail to pay premiums when they are due. Financial auditors may also verify that insurer underwriting and marketing personnel monitor the financial strength of producers and suppliers like systems vendors and actuarial and accounting service companies.

Producer Audits

Insurers that market their products through agents or brokers must periodically verify that their producers are observing the terms of their contracts. Producer contracts typically define producer authority to bind coverage, specify how premiums should be collected from customers, and describe how premium will be paid to the insurer. In addition to verifying the agreements specified in the agency contract, the insurer might want to review application completion and adherence to underwriting guidelines.

Producer audits are usually conducted jointly by the marketing and underwriting management responsible for the geographic territory where the producer is located. The insurer's underwriting and marketing management review premium and loss data for each producer every year and use it to discuss past performance and future expectations with the producers. The expectations are usually defined in terms of written premium and profitability, which are results that both the insurer and the producer can monitor.

Data from producer audits help an insurer to compare the producer results with overall insurer results in the territory or state. If the producer's portfolio has a greater concentration of certain types of risks than is characteristic of most other producers, the insurer should learn the reasons for the differences. If the producer's loss ratio is higher than the insurer's average in a particular line of business, that might also be an area for further data collection and analysis. Comparing changes in producer audits conducted at different times might reveal problems in achieving agreed upon levels of growth, profitability, or adherence to underwriting guidelines.

Audits of Underwriting Practices

Underwriters are customarily given specific written authority for premium, exposure size, and risk characteristics. Underwriting practices audits typically gather data about the following:

- Comparison of premium and loss results with goals for each underwriter
- Review of policy files to determine the thoroughness of application completion and file documentation
- Verification of the appropriateness of underwriter authority limits
- Verification that underwriting guidelines are understood and followed
- Verification that underwriting referral and processing procedures are followed

Those conducting the audit then interpret the data to determine whether the observed practices ensure the achievement of profit and growth goals. Although strict adherence to underwriting guidelines might be effective for lowering loss ratios, an inflexible approach to decision making might reduce the flow of business unnecessarily. If loss ratios are lower than goal when premium goals are not met, strict underwriting guidelines might be negatively affecting the flow of business. Although profitable loss ratios are generally more important than achieving an arbitrary written premium goal, underwriters are often expected to contribute to achieving both premium and loss ratio goals. Underwriting practices audits are a source of information that helps to assess this important insurer function.

The underwriting practices audit should summarize data collected by those conducting the audit and provide recommendations based on information developed from the data. Follow-up review is usually scheduled when additional data will be sampled to verify that underwriters have carefully considered the prior audit recommendations and that reasonable justification exists if recommendations were not implemented. Underwriting practices audits can sometimes reveal needed changes in underwriting guidelines, product features, work flow, and information systems.

Auditing Underwriting Practices: A Case Study

Assume that you are the underwriter of a portfolio that had $6 million in premium at the beginning of last year, and your premium goal for last year was to increase premium 10 percent while maintaining a 60 percent loss ratio. If your company had an expense goal of $1.85 million (28 percent of premium), the expectation inherent in the goal was that a 12 percent profit (100 – 60 – 28 = 12), or $792,000, would be achieved on $6.6 million in premium.

On the other hand, if you achieved a 59 percent loss ratio but did not achieve any premium growth, your company would probably still have spent $1.85 million in staff costs and advertising expenses trying to achieve the premium goal. But that amount must be compared with a lower premium ($6 million) than expected, so the expense ratio would be 31 percent. The combined loss ratio and expense ratio would be 90 percent (59 + 31 = 90), so the underwriting profit would be 10 percent (100 – 90 = 10) instead of 12 percent, as the goal stated. The 10 percent profit is calculated on a lower amount ($6 million), so your company's profit would be $600,000, or $192,000 less than goal.

To offset premium that is lower than planned, your organization would need to reduce expenses by an equal amount ($192,000), which would be greater than a 10 percent reduction in expenses. A 10 percent reduction in expenses is a dramatic reduction to accomplish in one year, particularly if the need for the reduction is not apparent until well into the year.

This discussion is not intended to discourage underwriters from achieving loss ratios better than goal. However, underwriters, customer service representatives (CSRs), and producers should realize that insurers must achieve both premium and loss ratio goals to achieve profit goals. Portfolios that have achieved the profit objective are usually not severely criticized, even if specific premium and loss ratio targets are not entirely achieved. However, when profit goals are missed, a close examination of the reasons is required. Understanding data and information sources is critical for identifying deviations from expected results and determining corrective action.

Regulatory Audits

When an insurer cannot meet the obligations of its policies, regulators are criticized for not recognizing the insurer's difficulties before they became serious. When losses must be paid from state insurer guaranty funds, claim settlements are sometimes delayed, and all insurance rates within the state might need to be increased to fund the failed insurer's inability to pay its losses.

Consequently, regulators are concerned that insurers maintain financial strength and the ability to pay customer claims.

In addition to requiring quarterly financial reports, as discussed earlier in this chapter, regulatory personnel typically perform on-site audits every three to five years of all insurers domiciled in their jurisdictions. For efficiency, one state's regulatory authority sometimes accepts the evaluation summary from an audit conducted by a regulatory audit team from another state.

Sometimes repeated customer complaints or a series of fines imposed by regulators triggers an audit. An audit can focus on gathering data about a particular financial issue, such as how one insurer of a group is reinsured by the assets of the other insurers in the group, or it can involve a detailed analysis of data such as claim response time.

Besides financial strength, customer complaints, and noncompliance issues, regulators are also concerned about social issues like rate equity and insurer responsiveness to customer inquiries. Insurers treat regulatory audits with great seriousness and frequently monitor the categories of data they anticipate to be of interest to regulators on a voluntary and regular basis.

Claim Audits

Claim service office managers routinely review claim files to assess claim personnel performance. In addition, representatives of insurer claim corporate departments perform periodic internal audits of claim files and procedures. Among issues of concern to insurers in claim audits are the following:

- Correctness of coverage, liability, and damage assessments
- Thoroughness of claim investigation
- Appropriateness and completeness of claim file documentation
- Accuracy of initial and subsequent case reserves
- Reasonableness of service time
- Observance of claim handling authority
- Appropriateness of diary or follow-up action

The type of data needed to perform a claim audit is commonly available in paper claim files and in electronic claim records. Insurers can choose to review claim file data by line of business, coverage, type of claim, geographic territory, claim office, employee, or many other methods of sorting data. Random file reviews are also conducted to identify general trends. The objective of claim audits is to review sufficient data to understand how effectively the claim operation is meeting the organization's and its customers' expectations for quality claim service. For claim files that are primarily maintained in paper form, copies can be made and shipped to auditor locations for review. To minimize costs, auditors often travel to the location of the paper files. Organizations that electronically store complete claim records can sample claim files created anywhere in the organization from most computer terminals at any time. Insurers with electronic claim files can also choose to perform claim audits on a continuous basis, increasing the possibility that deviations from expected performance will be identified early and that corrective action can be taken.

Operational Audits

Operational audits are similar to and sometimes combined with audits of underwriting practices. They typically involve collecting and evaluating data that detail work flow and information system usage. Insurers frequently define work methods and procedures to establish uniform processing among the various jobs their employees perform. Organizations with many branches reporting information among offices must ensure that similar information is being recorded and reported to guarantee that corporate statistics are consistently compiled.

Input processing sequences are important for correctly recording information in insurer databases. Customer billing procedures should be consistent so that cancellation practices are uniform and comply with regulatory requirements. Operational audits collect and analyze data that verify that procedures are being followed. Procedures should be revised when needs demand, particularly if customer service can be improved.

Summary

This chapter reviewed the types of data that insurers collect and how they use that data to develop useful information. Insurers use data and information to satisfy the demands of many groups, including regulatory authorities; owners and other stakeholders, including policyholders; and management and employees.

Regulators require that insurers report statistical and financial data that provide information about the insurers' financial solvency and marketing practices. Owners and other stakeholders are also interested in financial data; in addition, they request operational information that reveals how efficiently the insurer is functioning. Because management and employees need information to do their jobs, they interact with the information most frequently.

Much of the data that insurers collect results from economic events. Insurers have established accounting procedures to ensure that records are made whenever an economic event occurs. Like all businesses, insurers want to account for their revenue, obligations to others, and profits.

Information systems can be either manual or electronic. Regardless, the cycle for processing information consists of four steps:

1. Collecting data
2. Classifying data
3. Transforming or processing the data into information
4. Producing reports summarizing results

To determine whether they are achieving their expected results, businesses generate and study reports such as exception reports, processing reports, production reports, and special or ad hoc reports.

Managing data to develop useful information requires answering these questions:

- How are the data recorded?
- Which items of data can be accessed?
- What could the data be used for?
- Who can best use the data?
- What happens to the organization when the data are used?

Besides monitoring results for premium, losses, and expenses, insurers need information to meet requirements of statistical reporting agencies, to maximize administrative processing capabilities, to evaluate and improve work flow, to assess customer satisfaction, to monitor employee performance, and to audit procedural and regulatory compliance.

Chapter 2

Acquiring, Evaluating, and Monitoring Information

Between 1985 and 1995, entrepreneurial firms, organizations capable of identifying and responding to rapid changes in the business environment, dominated the creation of new jobs. Even though 50 percent of new businesses fail within the first five years of their operation, surviving new operations have generated almost all of the new jobs since 1980. Between 1980 and 1990, "the Fortune 500 companies eliminated 3.4 million new jobs while companies with less than 500 employees created more than 13 million new jobs."[1]

Some of those new jobs are in low-salaried, low-skill service work in food service, health care, retail sales, and maintenance. Others are in the knowledge or information businesses like insurance, finance, accounting, investments, and law. The latter types of jobs require employees who have good language, math, and interpersonal skills, basic familiarity with computers, and the capacity to adapt to change. Frequently, the new jobs in knowledge or information businesses require employees with the ability to access, interpret, and communicate information. Those skills are typically not required of mass production and manufacturing employees, and that difference represents a fundamental change in American employment. Working in reasonably well-paid jobs depends increasingly on possessing the abilities to access and interpret data, identify how data can be used to create useful information, and independently recognize how information can be applied to achieve organizational objectives.

Property and liability insurance organizations are good examples of entities that produce a knowledge, or information, product rather than a manufactured product. They also employ over 600,000 knowledge workers in the United States alone. Agencies and brokerages employ an additional 700,000.

Management practices are also changing. Command and control approaches to supervision may be appropriate for managing large numbers of employees performing repetitious tasks. But if employees are expected to exercise independent judgment, even within narrowly defined parameters, managers must use care not to impair employee decision making with excessive controls. Consequently, many of the traditional control approaches to management are counterproductive in highly competitive knowledge businesses, like insurance. As customers increasingly expect prompt decisions and fast service from knowledge workers (such as insurer customer service and claim personnel), management must grant greater authority to employees.

Adding to the demand for fast service is customer pressure for low-cost products and services. If employees can respond to customers with minimal management referral, many management positions can be eliminated. Consequently, employees who work in knowledge businesses, where information is the product, are increasingly expected to understand how to gather, record, and access data and to communicate information effectively, with little or no supervisory assistance.

Process Improvement

Organizations are committed to improving both the efficiency of their work and their ability to continuously satisfy customer needs. Information technology played a major role in the 1980s and 1990s in motivating organizations to reexamine their work processing procedures. In some cases, steps of processes like insurance rating and policy assembly were reassigned from manual processing to electronic systems processing.

Electronic systems processes of the 1960s and 1970s helped improve insurer efficiency. Personal computer-based (PC-based) systems greatly increased the number of processes that could be performed electronically and expanded the availability of information to all personnel with access to a personal computer. Additional efficiencies have also been achieved by organizations that reevaluated all of their processes, including those that the availability of sophisticated electronic processing did not directly affect. By integrating an evaluation of overall work procedures with efficiencies gained from electronic information systems, some organizations reduced the number of processing steps for some operations by 70 percent or more.

Improved simplicity of handling has shortened the time required to process insurance applications, changes, customer inquiries, and claims. Electronic storage and retrieval of data improved the ease with which insurers could access customer and claimant information. That further improved service and simultaneously raised customer and regulator expectations for prompt insurer responses. The efforts of insurers during the 1980s and 1990s to improve their processing efficiency and customer responsiveness were often described as quality improvement efforts. But many organizations besides insurers also focused on improving their efficiency and customer focus. The 1980s were a time of transition: from an era in which profits were substantial and customer choices were limited to an era in which profits were significantly less per unit of product sold and customer options were expanded dramatically. By the 1990s, efficient operations and quality service were no longer added values that companies could use to distinguish their products and services. They became requirements.

In the 1980s, businesses began to look for radical changes in their operations that could provide immediate and dramatic improvements in their efficiency, customer service, and product definition. Organizations began to expect their managers and employees to continually consider methods of redesigning the company in response to market opportunities and customer demands. Efforts to make radical change in business operations to achieve breakthrough results were labeled as reengineering, process innovation, and core process redesign. Michael Hammer and other management theorists began describing a new world for business in which three Cs (customers, competition, and change) are the driving factors for success: "Companies created to thrive on mass production, stability, and growth can't be fixed to succeed in a world where customers, competition, and change demand flexibility and quick response."[2]

That attitude signaled a major change in the way organizations viewed their businesses. Companies in the new business environment "are not asset portfolios, but people working together, to invent, sell, and provide service."[3]

In this new business environment, insurers need managers and employees who can respond to those challenges by understanding their products and customers and recognizing the need for changes and adaptability. The success of organizations, even in businesses based on agricultural trade and bartering, has always depended on the ability of the organization's employees to collectively produce something that is valued in the market. However, mass production, industrial organizational models with many divisions of labor and diffused responsibility among many levels of hierarchy, can easily cause employees to lose sight of the importance of creating a product customers will want.

In continuously adaptive business environments, market responsiveness is essential for survival. It requires accurate and continually updated information about customers, competitors, and regulators. It also requires employees who can quickly identify what information is needed, access it, interpret it, and respond appropriately. To ensure that they are responding appropriately, employees will increasingly need to compare their own performance with reasonable goals and assess the effects of their performance on the organization's ability to succeed. They will also need to continuously evaluate an ever-increasing volume of information.

Employee Environment

Individuals prepare for careers by completing some minimum level of learning. For those who work in the insurance business, that has historically included, as a minimum, a high school education, basic math and language skills, and a minimal ability to communicate orally and in writing. Increasingly, as access to information and customer expectations increase, individuals who work in insurance are expected to have at least some post-secondary education, and many acquire professional learning during their first few years of working for an insurer or insurance producer. For years, insurance professionals have learned about their business's skill requirements and operations by attending formal classes, seminars, and training sessions, many of which are provided by insurers, agencies, brokers, and nearby colleges and schools. Many insurance professionals have also used correspondence and electronic methods of study now described broadly as distance learning.

Many people learn effectively by exchanging ideas with a class leader and other members of a class. Such learning experiences are beneficial because they provide structured review of key points and opportunities to discuss complex issues. Consequently, classroom forms of learning will probably continue to play an important role in the way the insurance business improves the qualifications of its employees.

Reference sources, such as rating rules, premium calculations, technical specifications, copies of insurance contracts, state regulations, and legal and statutory references, once available only in paper form, are now often available from electronic files. From such files, insurer employees gain rapid access to information that might otherwise have required hours or days of research through paper documents and reference manuals. Descriptions of products and marketing territories, agent profiles, and decision referral networks are examples of the types of information that can easily be accessed electronically.

Educational material can also be provided electronically. Distance learning experiences once confined to textbook and workbook practice increasingly use electronic data sources to deliver educational products. Electronically delivered or facilitated courses are now available from both traditional and nontraditional institutions of higher learning throughout the world. Students can interact with faculty and other students using electronic telecommunication technology that provides new access to learning.

Links to Other Information

Besides affording more convenient storage and delivery of information, electronic data permit the creation of links to other data sources. For example, an underwriter reviewing an electronic application for a commercial auto liability policy on a lumber mill might want to check the insurer's underwriting guidelines to determine whether the particular risk is eligible. The underwriter could instantaneously switch from the electronic application to an electronic version of the company underwriting manual or other data available through the Internet. Many insurers are already exploring the opportunities such capability provides. If the underwriter also wishes to review unique exposures common to lumber mills, a link might be available from the underwriting guide to an electronic library containing descriptions of generic characteristics representing thousands of categories of businesses. Those descriptions might be linked to inspection ordering forms so that the underwriter can immediately request a loss control representative to inspect specific aspects of the applicant's business operation. These and other changes made possible by information systems have altered the nature of many insurer jobs.

The availability of large amounts of data that can be sorted rapidly, combined with customer expectation for rapid service, is likely to increase the importance of electronic information access in the future. It has been predicted that information technologies will change the nature of tasks performed by 90 percent of the U.S. workforce by 2010.

Insurance professionals must recognize that job descriptions are likely to continue changing and become even more demanding. For survival under such conditions, insurance employees must continually upgrade their skills. Those who provide learning experiences for insurance professionals, both those within insurer human resource departments and those who provide professional development curriculum and competency assessment, will need to take advantage of evolving information delivery systems to help insurance professionals meet the challenges of changing learning needs.

Framework for Evaluating Information

Under the industrial work model, managers with relatively exclusive access to information make decisions to establish and achieve organizational objectives. Many insurers still operate under an industrial work model, and many are highly effective with that approach. However, the increasing consumer and regulator demand for greater insurer efficiency has motivated insurers to minimize expenses, which has resulted in fewer middle managers, fewer secretarial and administrative employees, and greater responsibility for accomplishing necessary work among the employees who remain. Electronic data files have facilitated redistribution of work by providing more employees with direct access to necessary information that, under industrial organizational models, would have been restricted to management. Consequently, many insurers have redefined jobs to require employees to access and interpret data quickly with little or no supervisory assistance. Many of the redefined jobs also require language, math, and interpersonal skills that were less important in previous work environments, where each employee's responsibilities were more limited.

Upper management makes decisions about how to distribute responsibilities among employees, but accountability for satisfying the responsibilities is typically assigned to underwriters, marketers, administrators, and customer service personnel who interact directly with customers. The following list is a framework for evaluating an insurer's information management needs:

- Identifying needed data and sources
- Converting data to information
- Deciding who can best use information
- Assessing costs
- Verifying accuracy and consistency of data

Identifying Needed Data and Sources

Most insurers have become competent at collecting data that satisfy financial and statistical reporting requirements. Data describing written and earned premium, incurred losses, premium, loss reserves, and expenses are generally available. Consequently, most insurers can answer questions about how well their written premium meets their objectives, whether their losses are normal at some point in time, and whether expenses are less than expected. However, few insurers can readily answer the following types of questions:

- How are customers evaluating a product or service this week?

- What are producers most concerned about today?
- How are financial markets affecting policyholders' surplus this afternoon?
- What are key competitors doing this morning?
- What customer needs are likely to emerge tomorrow?
- What customer needs are likely to become less important tomorrow?

These are the types of questions that highly responsive and adaptive organizations can answer. Data are available to answer these questions, but few insurers assign importance to collecting and interpreting the data. As the following scenario suggests, however, asking and answering those types of questions can have significant business implications.

Surveying Customers: A Case Study

The Jackson-Crawford Insurance Company wants to know how its customers are evaluating its products and services this week. Its marketing department designs a short customer survey, identifies 500 customers who requested a change over the last six months, and contracts with a customer survey organization to contact those customers by phone to ask them the survey questions. One question asks about the ease with which the customer could get through on the insurer's toll-free phone line. Another question asks about the courtesy with which the customer was treated. A third question asks the customer what the insurer might have done better in handling the request.

An insurer that perceives itself as needing to respond to future customer needs might subscribe to magazine or Internet clipping services that search for new products requiring special insurance treatment. For example, computerized trip planning/mapping devices that use satellite navigation technology are increasingly available for installation on upscale private passenger autos. An insurer that perceives a market niche for itself in selling private passenger auto coverage to owners and lessees of upscale vehicles might design coverage especially for damage to navigation devices. Insurers with employees capable of searching Internet resources can probably identify such product and service opportunities without clipping services.

Insurers, like other businesses, recognize the need to access data relevant to their daily operations. However, each insurer defines its operations differently. Some insurers define their products and services narrowly. For example, an insurer might decide that it is a specialist in providing homeowners coverage to owners of single family homes in a limited geographic area within one state. In some stable markets, that may be sufficient to ensure success.

Aggressive, highly adaptive insurers are likely to perceive their business in broader terms. For example, AIG perceives itself as a collection of small, adaptive financial services businesses. Many of those businesses sell conventional insurance contracts, but the organization has earned a reputation as being innovative and willing to consider risks typically rejected by many equally well-respected insurers. The broader self-definition of companies like AIG, Chubb, and CIGNA suggests that they would need a greater range of data to make decisions than would insurers selling homeowners insurance in one or two counties.

Detailed analysis of data needs and sources is beyond the scope of this text. However, insurance professionals should recognize the relationship between their organization's business objectives and the changing market in which they operate. To adapt to change, organizations must identify their data needs, determine how to access the data, and then collect and evaluate the data they have accessed. Emerging needs for data, unlike established needs, often require facts that insurers have not collected previously. That means finding new sources of data, perhaps from sources not customarily associated with the management of insurance operations.

For example, an insurer with an objective to market windstorm property coverage in Puerto Rico might need, but not have, detailed weather data showing fifty-year storm tracks for the area. Such data are likely to be available from a government or aviation weather monitoring source or from a software vendor that has accessed such data for other possible users. For insurers, identifying the need for particular data and selecting an appropriate source are likely to be crucial in determining coverage limits, pricing, and underwriting guidelines, as well as for assessing surplus capacity and for negotiating reinsurance terms.

Converting Data to Information

Identifying the needs for and sources of data is the first step in evaluating information. However, since data are only a collection of facts, someone must decide how collected data can best be used to provide the information that facilitates the insurer's decision making. For example, data related to windstorms collected over a fifty-year period in Puerto Rico are likely to contain detailed tracking of storm travel, locations of storm landfall, recorded wind velocities, effects on tides, values of property on land located within the first ten feet above mean sea level, average property damage, and many other facts. For meaningful information to be derived from those facts, the interrelationships among the items of data must be analyzed and interpreted.

Developing Information From Facts: An Example

One likely relationship exists among wind velocity, rising tides, and property values exposed to loss. After reviewing fifty years of weather, tide, and property damage data, the insurer might learn that property damages are greatest when tides rise ten feet or more. The insurer might also learn that tides rise ten feet when wind velocities exceed 110 miles per hour. If the insurer learns that, each year, on average, two storms with wind velocity over 110 miles per hour occur, it could estimate the frequency of storms that might produce major property damage. If it further discovered from the data that locations of storm landfall were distant from major inhabited areas in five of every ten years, it would anticipate less damage than if storms struck densely populated areas every year. So weather, tide, and property damage data could be useful to insurers in determining their willingness to offer windstorm property coverage.

An insurer interested in learning how satisfied its customers are might survey one in ten customers who request a policy change. Customer opinions about the insurer's telephone response time, the courtesy of the customer service representative, and the ease of handling could be collected. In addition, the insurer could ask for the date and time of day the customer called the insurer. If it learns from analyzing the data that customers are least pleased with service received when calling between 11:00 A.M. and 2:00 P.M., the insurer might investigate why service appears to deteriorate between those hours. Similarly, the insurer might learn that service is better on Mondays than on Fridays. This use of information might motivate the insurer to further investigate the difference.

Deciding Who Can Best Use Information

In addition to understanding how to derive useful information from collected data, insurers must consider which functions within their organization can best use the information that has been identified. For example, an insurer that uses storm tracking data to predict potential property damage from windstorms might make that information available to underwriters, producers, and actuaries in order to help guide the selection and pricing of risks. An insurer that assesses customer opinion might distribute that information among customer service representatives to give them a better understanding of how customers perceive their efforts.

Evaluation of information often generates requests for additional information. For example, suppose the customer service representatives decide to use the customer survey information to improve their service. To better understand why customers perceive that service is slower during the middle of the day and on Fridays, they might begin collecting data to quantify the number of phone calls received during each hour of the day and on each day of the week. The evaluation of that additional data might quantify the number of additional employees (or telephone lines) that should be available during peak call times. When useful information is made available to those who can readily apply it in their work, improvements in service and efficiency can result.

Similarly, an insurer that evaluates customer survey information indicating a need for improved service might use that information to change its operations and achieve a breakthrough advantage over its competition. For example, one large insurance company gathered data about the procedures followed in processing small personal auto collision and other-than-collision claims. Although claim representatives were traditionally responsible for verifying the amounts of customer losses, the company's claim processing data revealed that claim representatives usually accepted the customer's repair estimate in determining the amount of small first-party private passenger auto losses. The insurer decided to omit the company inspection portion of the claim investigation on certain types of losses and permit customers to adjust their own claims by simply obtaining a repair estimate and sending it to the company. That radical departure from the usual company procedure dramatically reduced the time needed to settle many first-party losses and speeded claim settlement. Although that procedural change could have been made based on manual or paper claim data, electronic access permitted the review of large numbers of claims in relatively little time. That added credibility to the analysis and facilitated decision making.

Assessing Costs

Any risk can be insured profitably at some price. Whether customers are willing to pay that price is another matter. Similarly, the data needed to provide sufficient information for decision making can usually be accessed. However, the expected benefits may not offset the cost of obtaining and interpreting the data. Comparisons of expected costs and benefits are as important to decisions about accessing data as such comparisons are in other management decision making.

Insurer management has an obligation to owners and other stakeholders to ensure that the organization's assets are used in the most efficient manner. That includes choosing among sources of data. For example, replacement of legacy systems (described later in this chapter) with PC-based systems would improve an insurer's ability to distribute detailed customer underwriting, premium payment, and loss data among employees with PCs. That could be an important improvement worth an investment of many millions of dollars to an insurer operating in many states, selling multiple products, and using several distribution methods. However, an insurer selling only one or two products in a limited area of a single state might have sufficient access to data using existing mainframe-based systems and terminals. A small company that meets its processing needs with terminals might be unable to justify a $1 million investment in a PC network.

However, even a small company that chooses not to make large investments in computer systems could benefit from accessing additional types of data. For example, it might want to monitor competitor pricing of similar products. One option to access such data would be to routinely send an underwriter to the state insurance department to review competitor product, rate, and rule filings and financial statements. Another option might be to subscribe to rate comparisons available in print or disk or other electronic format. A third option, for insurers that market through producers, might be to form an agents' council that could meet quarterly to discuss changes in the competition. Each of these options would provide data useful in assessing market competition, but each involves different costs (both monetary and in terms of employee and management time). Management must evaluate all of the costs likely to accompany accessing data to determine whether the likely benefits are sufficient to justify the investment.

Cost decisions involving access to data can be crucial in product development and marketing planning. For example, physical inspections are one form of data insurers like to obtain in the underwriting process. However, the cost to perform physical inspections of average-value residential risks is generally prohibitive. An inspection that costs $50 could represent 25 percent or more of the annual homeowners or dwelling fire premium for some residential property policies. Such a cost might be difficult for insurers to justify, even though the information gained would be helpful in assessing exposure to loss and adequacy of pricing. On the other hand, an insurer that specializes in insuring high-value residences with replacement costs of $500,000 and above might have average annual premiums in excess of $5,000 per policy. Such an insurer might easily justify a physical inspection costing $200.

Decisions affecting how much and what types of data to obtain are becoming increasingly important as organizations define unique market niches for themselves. For example, an insurer with a commitment to satisfy the needs of many customers located in multiple countries might justify the cost of a full-time research department that investigates and monitors daily the economic, political, financial, and market trends in many countries. Although the annual cost of maintaining a department responsible for gathering and interpreting data could reach well into the millions of dollars, insurer management might determine that the international risk of its operation demands access to the type of data such a department could provide.

Multiple sources of data can often aid product, pricing, underwriting, and financial decision making. The cost must be weighed against the expected benefits to be received from the data. Included in the cost assessment should be not only the expenses associated with obtaining the raw data, but also the expenses associated with converting it into usable information. That requires assessing expenses such as computer hardware, programming requirements, additions to personnel, special training for existing personnel, and the salaries of employees who will be expected to invest time in gathering and interpreting the data.

Should the assessment reveal that the cost to access the needed data will exceed the insurer's expected benefit (even given several years to offset costs), management might decide not to obtain the required data. That decision could result in subsequent decisions to postpone development of some products or to avoid them entirely. However, a comprehensive evaluation of the costs and benefits associated with a particular data need often results in quantifying expected benefits. If the expected benefits are insufficient to warrant obtaining the originally required data, knowledge of the specific value of benefits could help quantify a budget that would be justifiable. Given a well-defined budget to acquire necessary data, management might locate alternative, lower-cost sources. Management's objective is typically to ensure the efficient use of resources. That usually means choosing options that minimize net costs while achieving the optimal net benefits for the organization.

Verifying Accuracy and Consistency of Data

Besides making data decisions that are economically efficient, insurer management is concerned that data obtained are accurate and consistent over time. For new sources of data, care must be taken in making decisions before enough time has passed to verify the data's accuracy and consistency. For existing sources of data, the same types of data must be collected for all periods of time measured, and the methods of collection must be consistent.

New Sources

Although managers of any business would like to access proven, existing sources of data, such sources may not be available. The dynamic nature of markets, particularly global markets, often presents unique new problems and opportunities. Changing customer needs frequently signal factors in society, the economy, the global market, or elsewhere in the environment that previously did not exist, or existed in some significantly different way. Consequently, the data needed to evaluate a possible response may inherently lack accuracy and consistency. That lower level of accuracy and consistency (compared with established data sources) does not, however, mean that insurers should avoid responding to those changes. On the contrary, the insurance business should be particularly responsive to such unknowns since it exists primarily to accept transfer of risk from those unwilling to retain the uncertainty of loss. However, any management that makes decisions based on new data sources should recognize the unproven nature of any information drawn from those sources.

Insurance professionals should question the accuracy and consistency of new data sources not only to decide whether to offer a product, but also to quantify the credibility that can be assigned to the data. Furthermore, decisions based on new data impose a responsibility on management to closely monitor the continuing collection of data so that inaccuracies are identified as quickly as possible, evaluated, and incorporated into decisions affecting product design, pricing, or underwriting.

Existing Sources

Existing sources of data satisfy many insurer management needs. For stable organizations operating in relatively consistent markets, data for premium, loss, and expense records are typically collected and maintained with high levels of accuracy and consistency. Insurers that operate in stable environments often come to expect their assessments of past results and their forecasts of future results to be highly credible. Unfortunately, even effectively managed and highly detailed long-standing data sources can be of limited benefit when environmental factors change and data are combined or separated.

Environmental Changes

Many large personal property insurers have sold homeowners policies in Florida for many years, even though coastal Florida has always been highly exposed to windstorm loss. Insurer loss data collection and record keeping have been accurate and consistent. However, the property environment of coastal Florida has changed over the past twenty years, and many insurers did not adequately contemplate that change in the data collection and interpretation process. Over the past twenty years, residential property construction has greatly increased in Florida, particularly in coastal communities. Homeowners insurers that were pleased to have a growing Florida book of business may have been lulled into confidence based on past experience with Florida rate adequacy. As an increasing percentage of homes were built in coastal communities that are exposed to windstorm loss, Florida's homeowners insurance rates became increasingly inadequate. The existing loss data were accurate, and the method of collection was consistent. However, that consistency may have created an unwarranted level of confidence in the continuing usefulness of the data for determining needed rates. Reliance on the existing data source failed to adequately inform insurer decision making.

New Data From Existing Sources

Suppose Florida property insurers had begun, in 1970, collecting data that revealed the disproportionately high growth of housing construction in Florida's coastal communities compared with inland construction. By 1980, such data might have shown the magnitude of the trend leading to a dramatic increase in the percentage of residences exposed to windstorm loss. Recognizing that change, insurers might have been able to forecast the effect it would have on potential catastrophic loss from windstorm. Although that would not have ensured regulator approval of increased coastal property rates, insurers could have used the information to substantiate requests for rate increases. They might also have used such data to elevate public awareness and debate about the nature of construction codes in coastal communities. Over a period of years, insurers might have been able to obtain regulator support for increased property insurance rates or for a redistribution of rates among geographic territories exposed to differing degrees of windstorm loss.

Existing data that have proven accurate and consistent over time are important to insurer planning and forecasting. Data revealing long-term trends in premium growth and loss experience are particularly helpful in forecasting growth in policyholders' surplus and in anticipating incurred losses. However, even the best of existing data sources should be closely evaluated periodically to verify that the data are reflecting changes in the environment.

Data Combination

Besides changes in the environment, changes in the data collection process can also affect data from existing sources. Two changes are common: **data combination** and **data separation**. First, insurers sometimes form or join groups of insurers because of acquisitions, mergers, licensing agreements, and reinsurance pooling. Different insurers, particularly those once-unrelated independent companies, often define different ways of collecting and sorting their data. Different insurers also have systems that were designed at different times using different languages and procedures. When different systems are combined and data files are merged, mistakes can occur in the data conversion process. Although total premiums and losses and overall financial results are usually transferred accurately, the detailed minor lines of business summaries sometimes develop errors. When reviewing historical sets of data that contain merged data files, insurers should compare the merged data with the original data. Verifying similarity of input is one way to assess whether merged data are likely to be accurate.

Combining or Merging Data: A Case Study

Insurer A buys Insurer B and calls the merged company Insurer AB. Both insurers have sold workers compensation policies for over ten years. Insurer A's claim personnel have used accurate claim description codes that include, for each claim, which part of the claimant's body was injured. Insurer A has closely monitored the input of those codes and has used data about injuries to body parts in planning loss control programs with its customers. Unfortunately, Insurer B has not been as diligent as Insurer A in defining claim description codes. In fact, Insurer B has changed its claim description code system twice in the past ten years and has never included in its codes which body part was affected in losses.

Insurer A has used its accurate claim description codes to manage loss experience for its workers compensation business. It knew, for example, what percentage of its claims resulted from workers lifting materials, and it knew what percentage of lifting injuries resulted in injuries to employees' backs.

Because the new company, Insurer AB, wants to analyze all workers compensation losses in the combined portfolios of Insurer A and Insurer B and because Insurer B's statistics did not have accurate claim description codes for each outstanding loss, Insurer AB decides to determine the percentages each of Insurer A's claim description codes represented of all Insurer A losses and then to apply those percentages to the merged total of losses for both Insurer A and Insurer B. That facilitates cause of loss analysis of the combined Insurer AB portfolio of insurance risks, but it adversely affects the accuracy of the claim description codes for the portfolio that was formerly identified with Insurer A. Managers making decisions dependent on the accuracy of claim description codes will need to consider how the combination of Insurer A's and Insurer B's claim records affects the accuracy and consistency of the coded data.

Before the combination occurred, Insurer A's claim description code records were probably both accurate and consistent. Insurer B's claim description codes, before the combination, were of little use. However, if both Insurer A and Insurer B were insuring similar types of risks at similar rate levels and with similar underwriting guidelines, using Insurer A's distribution of codes for the combined portfolio of policies might be reasonable. It might also help Insurer AB to understand the performance of the merged portfolios of risks. Although the distribution of claim description codes for Insurer AB is an estimate, it is at least based on the accurate coding previously used by Insurer A. Consequently, the combined company might have a better understanding of losses in the former Insurer B's portfolio than Insurer B had before the merger. If both portfolios are nearly the same size in premium and losses, an estimate of the total might be a better management tool than certainty for half and no information for the other half. If the portfolio of former Insurer A represents a significantly larger percentage of the total Insurer AB portfolio than does the portfolio of the former Insurer B, Insurer AB might have great confidence in making judgments using the distribution of former Insurer A's codes for the merged portfolio. On the other hand, if Insurer A represents a small fraction of the merged Insurer AB total, less confidence would be warranted.

This discussion is not intended to suggest that merged data have no value, nor is it intended as a caution to avoid merging data sources. Combinations of data are common in business mergers and acquisitions. However, understanding the history of existing data helps analysts identify the data's strengths and weaknesses and in assigning credibility to information derived from the data. In the Insurer AB example, analysts would be confident in measures of loss causes for Insurer A's portfolio before the merger. They would be less confident in the accuracy of the merged historical data of Insurer AB causes of loss.

Data Separation

Organizations can choose to combine data among member companies or among divisions of a company in many ways and for many reasons. Similarly, separation of data might be advantageous for some organizations. The incompatibility of data may require separate data files and access methods. Each organization must determine its own data needs and data manipulation limitations. Whenever data are combined or otherwise adjusted to reflect different data collection and storage methods, management must recognize that the accuracy and consistency of the data can change. Potential inaccuracies and inconsistencies do not necessarily invalidate data, but they may limit the data's usefulness.

In the example of Insurer AB, in addition to combining the data, the data could be separated to isolate claim code records for the former Insurer A portfolio after the merger. That would preserve the accuracy of the set of claim description codes for the Insurer A business without preventing its use in estimating code distribution for the merged portfolio. Some insurers try to assign identifying codes when data are merged so that data can later be isolated on demand for analysis purposes. Insurance analysts also use such identifying codes to separate data when they suspect that inaccuracies and inconsistencies might have occurred when data were combined.

Information Sources and Performance Objectives

A primary use for data and information is responding to insurer performance objectives. Objectives are typically set at the following three broad levels:

- Strategic—long-term market forecasts, product development, and possibilities for acquisition or merger
- Tactical—short-term product distribution and profitability
- Operational—process-oriented objectives for billing, accounting, policy issuance, and claim handling

How those levels relate to management practices and organizational behavior is discussed in detail elsewhere in the CPCU 7 curriculum. This chapter is concerned primarily with how setting insurer objectives influences data and information needs and how performance is monitored and compared with insurer objectives. Three broad categories of information needs, unstructured, semistructured, and structured, closely correspond to the three categories of organizational objectives.

This text uses the terms "unstructured," "semistructured," and "structured" to suggest differences in the way that data are ordered. Because strategic or long-term objectives depend on estimates of data that are often external to the organization, the data tend to be general and relatively **unstructured**. Because tactical or medium-term objectives use data from both internal and external sources, the data are usually more well defined or more structured (**semistructured**) than data used for setting strategic objectives. Since operational objectives are concerned with daily processes, most of the data needed to establish objectives and monitor how well they are achieved are from internal sources and consequently are well defined or highly **structured**.

Strategic Objectives/Unstructured Information Needs

Strategic objectives concern management issues that affect periods longer than one year and sometimes as long as five years. Historical data over long periods are frequently assessed to make forecasts. Past insurer performance often suggests trends for the future. But strategic decisions are intended to help an organization position itself to take advantage of business opportunities that are likely, according to those who assess the future, but that have not yet occurred. Consequently, information used to define strategic objectives tends to be subjective assessments of various factors made by people knowledgeable about business and economic trends. **Strategic information** is the collective best guesses of the well-informed.

Strategic information affects long-term objectives and includes forecasts, economic assessments, and other estimates of the future.

Using Strategic Information: A Case Study

Insurer D sells workers compensation insurance in the southeastern United States. It would like to double its premium volume over the next five years. Insurer D's owners and senior managers have read about economic growth in the Southwest and believe they may be able to expand in Arizona and New Mexico. They hire a consulting economist who provides forecasts about expected business growth in those states. Insurer D's marketing experts travel to the Southwest to speak with prospective salespeople about growth opportunities. They study changes in local workers compensation laws and insurance rates, and they speak with local politicians to explore the likely future direction of the workers compensation laws. Senior management also meets with insurers currently writing workers compensation coverage in Arizona and New Mexico to learn about loss experience and unique characteristics of the territory. After collecting and evaluating a substantial volume of such unstructured and subjective information, Insurer D's senior managers establish a strategic objective. Whether the objective is reasonable depends on the accuracy and completeness of the information collected, the thoroughness with which it was analyzed, and how well it matches Insurer D's objectives.

Although strategic information is highly subjective and susceptible to error, it is typically the primary type of information used to make long-term plans. It is used for strategic marketing plans, as in the previous example of Insurer D, and in planning major long-term objectives like company acquisitions and mergers. For example, senior management at Insurer E might establish a strategic objective to evaluate two prospective company acquisitions annually. Information needed to support that objective includes communications from capital markets identifying prospective acquisitions, financial analyses of and sales forecasts for prospective acquisitions, comparisons of Insurer E's strategies with objectives of the prospective acquisition, long-term future sales projections for the acquisition, an assessment of the two companies' information systems, and additional subjective evaluations. Such information tends to be summarized, broad rather than focused, and involves data that are both external and internal to the organization developing the strategy. Consequently strategic information tends to be less structured than the types of information used in setting tactical and operational objectives.

Tactical Objectives/Semistructured Information Needs

Owners, stockholders, and directors who represent owners typically require those responsible for defining and achieving the strategic objectives to provide information about results. Reports to boards of directors might be made quarterly, monthly, or more frequently. Such reports are likely to include some subjective and relatively unstructured information, such as that used in defining strategic objectives. That information could be reports that senior management uses in determining strategic objectives or senior management narratives that describe key elements of the information used in making strategic decisions.

In addition to selected strategic information, boards of directors are likely to expect senior managers to provide more objective and structured information that permits a better assessment of the organization's performance in the current year. Such information supports tactical objectives.

> **Tactical information** affects medium-term objectives, such as within the next year, and includes measures of recent performance and trends suggested by the analysis of those measures.

For example, insurers establish annual, quarterly, and monthly objectives for written and earned premium, incurred losses, and expenses. Historical information is useful for identifying trends that can be studied to set further tactical performance objectives. By monitoring **tactical information** monthly, weekly, or more frequently, insurers can identify which tactical objectives are being met or exceeded and locate deficiencies that can then be addressed with appropriate management action. Although much of the information used in establishing tactical objectives comes from inside the organization and is structured and finitely measured, like premiums, losses, and expenses, tactical objectives also require assessment of short-term competitor and regulatory issues. Consequently, although information needed to support tactical objectives is more internally focused than is the information needed for strategic objectives, it still requires some external information. Such information is less structured than the finite performance measures possible for internal information. As a rule, information used for tactical objectives is more structured than the information used for strategic objectives, but less structured than the information used for operational objectives.

Operational Objectives/Structured Information Needs

Operational information is perhaps the most structured kind of insurer information since it affects such activities as daily policy processing, claim payments, policy premium billing, and accounting records. Insurers typically expect to be able to access operational information on an as-needed basis. For example, if a customer wants to know whether the insurer received a recent premium payment, the insurer would like to access the policy's premium payment status immediately. Operational information gives insurer personnel access to data that can be used to determine whether a new policy has been issued, whether a change has been made to an existing policy, or whether a claim payment has been processed.

Operational information affects daily process issues like application review, premium billing, claim payments, and document printing. It is used to assess how daily functions contribute to achieving long-term objectives.

Although insurers compare their operational performance with the performance of other insurers, most of the information needed to inform operational objectives comes from within the organization and is highly structured. It also tends to be more objective than subjective, more current than predictive, and more limited in range of issues covered. Insurer operational performance objectives commonly concern the number of days for policy issuance and endorsement processing and the number of hours between first notice of a claim until the insurer claim representative calls the customer. These are finite measures for which specific objectives can be established. Results can be compared with objectives, and deficiencies can be identified easily.

Results Monitoring

Besides using data and information to define performance objectives, insurers monitor and adjust performance to achieve objectives. Because performance objectives are set at strategic, tactical, and operational levels, insurers typically establish methods to monitor performance accordingly.

Results Monitoring for Strategic Objectives

Because strategic objectives depend on highly subjective, relatively unstructured, external, and broad types of information, insurers routinely challenge their existing assumptions based on such information. If senior managers established a strategic objective to expand marketing activity in new territories based on strategic information, they are likely to question the assumptions on which that decision was based until the shorter-term tactical results demonstrate that strategic results are being achieved or cannot be achieved. Until that occurs, they might seek updated annual or quarterly market and economic assessments, competitor analyses, and other external information that supports (or refutes) past information.

Results Monitoring for Tactical Objectives

Tactical objectives are semistructured and based on a greater proportion of internal information than are strategic objectives. Insurer management tends to have greater confidence in using internal rather than external information for assessing performance compared with objectives. Many insurers can access measurements of premium, losses, and expenses on demand, but almost all insurers produce monthly data summaries for such tactical objectives as written premium, earned premium, incurred losses, and expenses. The data are typically organized in printed reports or computer monitor displays of information to facilitate comparing data (such as premium, losses, and expenses) at different points in time and with objectives.

To compare actual results to tactical objectives, insurers are likely to monitor, for each of their lines of business, the following:

- Earned premium
- Written premium
- Paid losses
- Changes in reserves
- Underwriting expenses other than commissions
- Commissions

Insurers typically produce reports to help them monitor their premium, losses, and expenses. Such reports usually display the results for a particular period (current week, month, or year-to-date through the end of the period). In addition, reports often include the corresponding objective (for the same time period) for the result being measured. Such reports commonly show a comparison with a prior period. For example, a measure of results for February of the current year might include a comparison with results for February in the previous year. Alternatively, results for February in the current year might be compared with January in the current year. Monitoring information that describes tactical results is particularly important for adjusting an insurer's underwriting and marketing activities.

Comparing Data: A Case Study

Insurers with sophisticated electronic data access capability can construct comparisons of results according to a wide range of possibilities and can display comparisons in a variety of formats. Suppose the managers of hypothetical Enterprise Insurance have set a goal to increase written premium 8 percent over the prior year. They notice from their regular results monitoring that written premium for private passenger auto liability coverage for August is 10 percent higher than it was for the same month in the previous year. Enterprise's underwriters want to know why results differ from the objective. They could compare monthly written premiums for each of the twelve months between August of the previous year and August of the current year to determine the amount of increase in other months. Year-to-date comparisons could also be useful to assess cumulative premium growth.

Exhibit 2-1 is a portion of a typical insurer monitoring report that shows written premium for private passenger auto bodily injury liability. An insurer could use this information to monitor how well it achieves tactical objectives. Because it includes information that describes results in different time periods, the report can also indicate trends.

Exhibit 2-1
Tactical Results Monitoring Report—Enterprise Insurance

Private Passenger Auto Liability—August		
	Written Premium	Percent Change From Prior Year
Current Year	$33,000	+ 10%
Objective	$32,400	+ 8%
Prior Year	$30,000	+ 6%

The table shows results for one month, in this case, August of the current year. Such reports, whether printed or electronically displayed, can also be used to compare year-to-date results with year-to-date objectives and year-to-date results for the prior year. Reports can also describe results for a day, a week, a year, a specified number of days, a specified number of months over multiple calendar years, or year-to-date at any point in time. Flexibility of manipulating information in that way permits underwriters to understand the results being monitored.

Using the limited information in Exhibit 2-1, an underwriter could learn that premium in August of this year was 6 percent higher than premium in August in the prior year. The objective for the year's increase was 8 percent, but the actual increase was 10 percent. Because the report shows only the month of August, it does not reveal whether the greater-than-expected growth rate implies that the year-end premium result will also be greater than the objective. To answer that question, the underwriters will need to monitor cumulative information over a longer time, such as year to date. For example, the underwriters might obtain a report of year-to-date results (see Exhibit 2-2).

Exhibit 2-2
Tactical Results Monitoring Report—Enterprise Insurance

Private Passenger Auto Liability—August Year-to-Date		
	Written Premium	**Percent Change From Prior Year**
Current Year	$2,330,000	+ 8%
Objective	$2,329,560	+ 8%
Prior Year	$2,157,000	+ 7%

Exhibit 2-2 shows the written premium results for the same insurer for which results were illustrated in Exhibit 2-1. However, Exhibit 2-2 shows results for the eight months ending on August 31 (and through August in the prior year column) as opposed to showing the results only for August of the current year (and August of the prior year), as was the case in Exhibit 2-1. Observing the results over eight months reveals that year-to-date premium growth is only 8 percent and not 10 percent as in August alone. Eight-month results are very close to plan, with both the actual and objective written premium growth at 8 percent.

Also apparent from the year-to-date monitoring report is that the prior year increased by 7 percent over the year before. That information permits the underwriter to consider the 8 percent growth of the current year in perspective with prior-year growth. Although 8 percent is a greater rate of growth, it is not so much greater that the underwriter might doubt its reasonableness. The fact that it is the same as the objective suggests that the increase is consistent with what insurer management thought was possible. Furthermore, having achieved a total of 8 percent growth over eight months, the insurer will likely achieve its growth goal for the current year if it can maintain growth for the remaining four months. Further, if it averages 8 percent growth over the remaining four months, it will achieve its 8 percent year-end objective. By reviewing Exhibit 2-2, the underwriter would gain some confidence that the premium growth objective is being achieved (but not exceeded, as might have been suggested by the results for August alone) and that 8 percent growth for the rest of the year is reasonable to expect.

Examining Tactical Data More Closely

An examination of the individual monthly premium for each of the eight months of the current year compared with objectives would be useful in verifying whether growth is relatively stable (such as generally averaging between 7 and 9 percent growth each month). To review individual months, the underwriters would need to access information like that contained in Exhibit 2-1 for each of the eight months of the year. In examining the monthly premium, the underwriters might discover that growth is not stable. For example, they might discover that growth was 6 percent in January and February, 8 percent in March, 9 percent in April and May, and 10 percent in June, July, and August. If a similar increasing rate of growth was also characteristic of months of the previous year, and the monthly distribution of the year's premium is similar over time, it would suggest that although growth varies by month, the year-end growth rate objective of 8 percent is reasonable. However, if the growth rate in each month in the previous year was relatively stable, between 6 and 8 percent, the current-year trend of increasing growth rates might suggest that year-end premium growth will be greater than the eight-month increase of 8 percent. In that case, year-end growth might be as high as 10 percent.

Monthly measures that assess results for tactical objectives over time can also help underwriters identify seasonal trends in premium growth (losses, or expenses, if those are the tactical results being monitored). If the monitoring process reveals that unusual activity occurs in particular months, the insurer might want to contemplate the uneven monthly distribution in setting future monthly tactical objectives.

Results Monitoring for Operational Objectives

Information for monitoring operational objectives, in contrast with information used to monitor strategic and tactical objectives, tends to be highly structured, detailed, current, specifically related to daily performance issues, and concerned with events within the organization. Premium, losses, and expenses are among the categories of information monitored on a daily basis for operational as well as tactical performance reasons. However, information monitored for operational purposes emphasizes processing, or work flow, that contributes to the achievement of tactical and strategic objectives.

For example, operational items monitored to support strategic and tactical premium objectives might include the following:

- Whether premium received is deposited promptly
- Whether written premium amounts are accurately recorded as each application is processed
- Whether application information is accurately input
- Whether applications are promptly processed for policy issuance or referred to underwriters
- Whether underwriters promptly review applications, endorsements, and renewals
- Whether appropriate underwriting guidelines are followed
- Whether appropriate underwriting authorities are observed

Work in process reports, discussed in Chapter 1, can help insurers monitor operational performance. They are especially effective in monitoring the quantity of certain types of work and for assessing the time required to process applications, endorsements, and claims. Other methods of monitoring operations include electronically assisted audits (on-line processing activity or information system report summaries) and manual audits (operational procedures).

Electronically Assisted Audits

Organizations with on-line access can monitor the current status of applications, premium payments, customer contacts, endorsement processing, and claim settlements. Anyone with appropriate authorization can inquire how many items of work were received during any period of time, who worked on it, when they worked on it, how long it took to complete all of the necessary steps in the process, and the current status of any particular item. Such systems permit management and authorized employees to review individual performance, the performance of specific work units, and the results achieved by the entire organization.

Manual Audits

Organizations with manual systems can use procedural audits to collect data about the organization's work. Front-line supervisors perform random comparisons between input documents and output documents to verify input accuracy. Comparisons of risk characteristics described in applications can be compared with target risk profiles to verify whether underwriters are adequately adhering to insurer underwriting guidelines. Front-line supervisors and representatives of insurer underwriting management conduct such reviews.

Claim management performs similar reviews of sample work to collect data that verify appropriate claim handling. Supervisors and corporate customer service personnel periodically monitor telephone calls with customers for courtesy, accuracy, and promptness of response. Information developed from manual reviews of work samples is used to assess how well individual employees and work units are achieving operational performance objectives. That information is also used to refine training and education programs aimed at improving the achievement of objectives and to refine processing procedures and underwriting guidelines.

Access to Information

For centuries, insurers have employed knowledge workers who know how to record and retrieve, generally manually, data describing transactions. Those employees have exhibited skill at interpreting data to create information that is meaningful to customers. In the last quarter of the twentieth century, though, the speed with which data are recorded and retrieved and the extent to which electronic systems can facilitate the creation and distribution of useful information have changed dramatically. Two primary categories of electronic processing systems for recording data and accessing information have evolved thus far: **mainframe-based systems** and **PC-based systems**.

Mainframes are high-storage, high-processing-capacity computers to which terminals or PCs can be connected. They are particularly useful to insurers for statistical record keeping, financial analysis, and results comparisons over multiple years. Mainframes can also process individual policy and claim transactions, and, during the 1960s and 1970s, they were used extensively for that purpose. Early access to mainframe data was by use of terminals (sometimes called "dumb terminals" because they have no data storage or programming capability). Systems that depend on terminals to access mainframe data and input new data are called **mainframe-based systems**. Insurers that use mainframe-based systems must send and receive one item of data at a time. In contrast, **PC-based systems** use the memory and processing capability of PCs, instead of terminals, to interact with mainframes. PCs permit insurers to send and receive many items of data in files virtually simultaneously. PC-based systems greatly reduce the amount of time required to access and manipulate large volumes of information.

PC-based systems are also called client-server systems for the relationship between the user of information (the client) and the system serving the user's need (the server). These systems store data in a mainframe computer much like mainframe-based systems do; however, they permit access to mainframe data by copying mainframe files, sending them electronically to PCs (where data are adjusted and manipulated), and then returning the data files to the mainframe.

Mainframe-Based Systems

Insurers have made extensive use of mainframe-based systems since the 1960s, although many did not make large investments in systems until the late 1970s. Most insurers are still using information systems that evolved from their original systems, and most continue to depend on **mainframes** for at least their corporate statistical and financial information. However, few insurers depend on their mainframes for daily policy and claim processing as they did in the 1960s and 1970s. PCs and PC networks now perform much of daily data processing. PC and PC network data are subsequently edited and transmitted to the mainframe to update the organization's primary data records.

New programming languages and storage mechanisms have replaced early systems in many cases. Many programs written for early systems are written in computer languages that have become obsolete or obscure. Insurers that continue to depend on their mainframe-based systems (and some early PC-based systems) for daily policy and claim processing find it difficult to perform maintenance, such as insurance rating refinements, and to adapt to the changing demands of the insurance environment. For some early systems, few remaining employees have the skills required to repair the hardware or to understand the programming required by older system language.

Most systems today still depend on the large data storage and retrieval capability of mainframes. Mainframe-based systems are essential for many of the complex financial analysis processes that insurers require to analyze their results over many years. Further, the comparisons and analyses performed by insurance information monitoring and statistical organizations depend on large mainframe-based systems to sort and compare results from many insurers in all states. In addition, for insurers that limit their product offerings to one or two essentially identical products for which hundreds of thousands of identical transactions occur each year, the high-speed processing capacity of main-frame-based systems might be adequate for even their daily transactions.

However, insurers that offer many different products, whose customers require a wide range of coverages, or who experience a great variety of claims, typically require greater adaptability than mainframe-based systems provide. Conse-quently, for daily policy and claim processing, they depend more on modern PC-based systems that use local area networks (LANs) and wide area networks (WANs). Such systems provide rapid access to individual policy and claim records, which helps insurers meet the demands for coverage information. PC-based systems transmit data to insurer mainframes, updating existing statisti-cal and financial records so that the mainframe's capacity to process large numbers of complex and detailed transactions continues to benefit insurer efficiency. PC-based systems are better suited for most individual daily trans-actions. Further, PC-based systems use technology that is easily modified to meet changing pricing, coverage, and regulatory demands. Changes to main-frame-based systems, whether hardware or software, are more costly and time-consuming than most changes to PC-based systems.

The "Y2K" Problem

An example of the types of problems created by early systems is seen in the difficulties created for some insurers because their original systems failed to provide sufficiently large input fields to differentiate between a two-digit year and a four-digit year. When insurers recorded dates in the 1960s, mainframe computer memory capabilities were a fraction of the memory capability of some modern laptop computers. Businesses in the 1960s avoided using limited system memory whenever possible. One of the areas in which businesses economized on memory use was in recording dates. Dates are important in electronic systems because they trigger processes. Insurers use dates to trigger data indicating when coverage is effective and when coverage ends.

Ideally, eight characters should have been used for recording dates, in order to permit electronic records to recognize changes of centuries. However, many businesses decided to use only six characters for date records, two for the month, two for the day, and two for the year. These limitations caused concerns toward the end of the twentieth century about the capacity of computer programs to continue performing as expected after December 31, 1999. This is known as the "Y2K" problem for the year 2000 (2K).

The Y2K problem characterizes the types of limitations that occur when modern systems continue to depend on data coded for and stored in early systems, often referred to as **legacy systems** because subsequent systems inherit their strengths and weaknesses.

Legacy systems are computer systems designed to perform specific or discrete tasks for which later requirements change significantly. They are called legacy systems because an organization assumes their design limitations for many years.

If legacy systems limit access to data and, therefore, to usable information, why do so many insurers still use them? The answer has to do with cost and benefit. Insurers that market relatively few lines of business and that have a stable group of customers might not require frequent access to a great deal of data to manage their results adequately. For such organizations, the limited capabilities of a system installed in the 1980s might continue satisfying the organization's rating, policy issuance, claim, and statistical data needs well into the twenty-first century. If conversion to a newer system requires an investment of many millions of dollars, an insurer would need to evaluate whether the expected gains in efficiency or access to data are sufficient to warrant the cost. The cost of changing systems includes the following:

- New computer hardware
- Converting existing data from legacy systems to a new system
- Potential for data-entry mistakes in the conversion process
- Time required to test for accurate conversion
- Possible need to operate two systems simultaneously for two or more years during conversion
- Changes to manual work procedures
- Employee retraining
- Availability of competent systems technicians and trainers

On the other hand, if the current system is not functioning as the organization desires and if the potential benefits of converting to a new system are likely to offset the costs, a problem such as adjusting dates for the year 2000 might be a deciding factor in a decision to replace the existing legacy system.

Competitive as well as organizational issues affect the decision to select new systems. Is the existing system likely to meet customer needs for the foreseeable future? What are the risks if it does not meet customer needs? What advantages are competitors gaining from new technology? What needs for information access have existing systems not met?

PC-Based Systems

Problems with legacy systems concern more than how they limit an insurer's processing ability and access to data. The design of mainframe-based and early PC-based systems was fundamentally different from the design of modern PC-based systems. Early systems were designed as tools to perform specifically defined, or discrete, processes. For example, those systems performed well at rating policies, such as homeowners policies, that have limited rating variables. However, because those systems were designed to solve specific processing problems, many early systems required new programs to be written for processes that deviated from the process for which the original program was written. Some early insurer systems might, for example, require writing a new program for each of several homeowners rating tiers in a given state.

Object-oriented programming (OOP) is an approach to program design that uses preassembled, generic data modules containing sets of instructions that can be used for similar purposes. In conventional programming, every program instruction is written from scratch. Generic data modules, called objects, speed the process of writing computer instructions and therefore permit insurers to respond to changes more rapidly.

Certain characteristics of newer systems might be important to insurers in evaluating the continuing acceptability of their legacy systems. For example, an insurer that is displeased with the time required to make rate changes in an early legacy system might want to gain the advantages of **object-oriented programming (OOP)** approaches to system design. In OOP designs, the programs are generic or multipurpose. An OOP homeowners rating system is likely to be usable for rating many homeowners programs on multiple rating tiers and in multiple states or rating territories. With OOP, an insurer can adjust its rates in response to changing loss experience much more quickly than insurers with systems designed to perform discrete tasks. An ability to respond rapidly to changes might be a significant marketing advantage for an insurer that sells multiple rating tiers of a given product or that operates in multiple states. OOP designs could also reduce the cost of system changes by minimizing programming revision costs. Advantages of new systems designs, such as those provided by OOP, might be a factor in an insurer's decision to convert from an otherwise satisfactory legacy system.

Another problem with legacy systems is their tendency to be collections of multiple, separate, nonintegrated systems that were designed for separate functions (for example, claims, underwriting, policy writing, and statistical reporting). Because of their design, combining data from different systems is often difficult. For example, when claim records are recorded in one system and underwriting data are stored in another system, underwriters cannot easily access detailed claim information for underwriting policies. Similarly, claim representatives have difficulty accessing underwriting information that could help verify coverage details. Lack of access to information decreases an insurer's ability to understand the causes of its results and adversely affects decision making.

The operation of PC-based systems is fundamentally different from that of mainframe-based systems. Many early systems locate all data in the main-frame. To input or access data, employees use a computer terminal. Such terminals have none of the computing or data storage capability of a PC. Every item of data input on a terminal keyboard is transmitted separately to the mainframe over a communication line that is active during the entire trans-mission process. Similarly, an employee accessing data opens a file and requests specific sets of data from that file, one set at a time. A set of data might be ten input fields that appear in the top fourth of an insurance application form. That data set might then be displayed on the employee's terminal monitor.

The communication line between the employee and the mainframe file remains open during the entire transaction. The request for each set of data is sent from the terminal to the mainframe whenever a different set is needed. The mainframe sends each set of data to the terminal as it is requested. The connection between the employee's terminal and the mainframe during the file access process is like a telephone connection between two private tele-phone numbers. While one terminal is accessing data in a particular file, access to that file by other terminals is typically not possible. (When a terminal tries to access a file already in use, the mainframe typically sends a message to the inquiring terminal indicating that the file is temporarily unavailable.)

After a series of inputs or commands has been completed, the central com-puter is instructed to perform some process. The performance of that process by the mainframe usually restricts availability of data files. Consequently, all processing is usually delayed until demand for mainframe access is low, such as at night, to limit interruption of work. The success or failure of that process is later communicated to the employees who keyed the input. If the process is not successful, the need for correction is typically not known until the next day. Such processing is fairly slow by PC standards.

PC-based systems, like mainframe-based systems, store and retrieve information in a mainframe database, but the method used to access and adjust data is significantly different. Unlike terminals, PCs have substantial memory with which to store programming instructions and sets of data. Consequently, with a PC-based system, an employee can request from the mainframe a copy of the entire file, which can then be stored temporarily in the PC.

Faster Processing

The amount of time required to obtain a copy of the entire file from the mainframe is a fraction of the time required to access data from the mainframe one data set at a time. Because PC-based systems can access multiple mainframe data sources, the information available temporarily to employees on their PCs is likely to include all data the insurer has about its customers, including underwriting and claim history, account billing, producer information, pending changes, and any comments or notes (made by anyone in the organization) relevant to servicing a customer's needs. Because the mainframe's file is open only long enough to copy its contents (fractions of a second), access to additional copies of the same file can be provided virtually simultaneously from many PC locations. After an employee accesses the file, it is sent back to the mainframe to replace the previous record. The time to transmit the entire file to the mainframe, including changes made to it, is minimal compared with the time required to send changes one data set at a time.

Edits Performed at Each PC

Besides the time saved by PC-based processing, the PC's capacity (independent of the mainframe) to store programs and perform complex processes means it can perform edits on files copied from the mainframe while they are temporarily stored in the PC. A PC can perform the validation processes performed by the mainframe, permitting employees to know, as soon as they input a change, whether the computer will accept the change. They no longer need to wait for the mainframe to perform the data verification edits. Consequently, when employees send their adjusted copy of the file to the mainframe to become part of the central record, it has an extremely high probability of passing all edits, thus minimizing the error correction process.

Greater Compatibility With Other Systems

Another significant change that occurred in the accessibility of data in the PC-based environment was the commonality of software among different organizations. In early mainframe-based systems, each insurer typically developed its own unique system. Although such systems may adequately serve one organization's specific processing needs, the systems are not readily compatible with others' systems, or even with other systems within the same insurer. Unique systems make it difficult to communicate electronically among insurers, among insurer locations, and between insurers and entities to which data must be reported (such as state insurance departments and data collection services such as Insurance Services Office). Further, mainframe-based systems cannot easily communicate with agency and broker systems, many of which are PC based. As insurance customers increasingly expect to communicate directly with insurers using PCs, insurers that rely on mainframe-based systems for their daily transaction processing and file access will have greater difficulty establishing the expected level of communication.

Consolidating Similar Processes

As the methods of data storage and retrieval become more standardized, communication improves among entities involved in the insurance business. New possibilities for achieving improved efficiency are also identified. For example, assume that ten insurers currently maintain separate data management departments. One of them could provide that service for all ten more efficiently. If they have concerns about privacy and preservation of exclusive information, they might consolidate data management under one separate servicing company. If privacy and anti-trust concerns can be minimized, a few data archiving services could assume some of the policy and claim recording responsibilities for many companies much the way a few independent companies currently provide property inspections, loss control reports, claim adjusting service, motor vehicle operator histories, and retail credit reports.

As PC-based data management evolves and becomes more standardized throughout the insurance business, the opportunities for consolidating insurers, creating strategic alliances among different entities, starting joint ventures, and building virtual insurance entities are likely to increase dramatically.

Outsourcing is the performance of needed functions by nonemployees, usually under contract.

Outsourcing

Outsourcing occurs when an organization arranges for necessary services to be provided by one or more individuals who are employees of an independent service-providing entity. Outsourcing is usually arranged under contracts that specify the terms of the transferred functions or activities and the compensation the contractor will be paid for performing the services. For example, many insurers employ loss control representatives to visit insured businesses, identify hazards, verify the insurer's previous assessment of loss exposures, and assess the insured's compliance with safety improvement recommendations. Independent loss control inspection services are available on a contract basis to accomplish the same objectives that employee loss control inspectors provide. Some insurers contract for such services exclusively for their loss control inspection needs, and others use these services when their loss control employees temporarily cannot handle large volumes of work.

Outsourcing offers the following advantages over performing the same functions with employees:

- *Flexible capacity to deliver services.* Insurers need only purchase as much of a contractor's service as they need and may terminate that service when they no longer need it.

- *Potentially lower cost.* Organizations that specialize in delivering a narrow range of services can often develop efficiencies that others cannot.

- *Greater expertise.* Specialist organizations might develop greater knowledge about that particular service than organizations that also perform many other functions.

- *Transferal of employer–employee obligations.* Employees of the contractor are not employees of the entity choosing to outsource that service. Therefore, their vacation, health insurance, workers compensation, and unemployment costs are the responsibility of the contractor.

Although outsourcing offers many advantages, it also creates some potential disadvantages, including the following:

- *Lack of direct control.* Since contractors are independent, their scheduling and methods of performing services cannot be directly controlled.

- *Possible inconsistency in the level of service provided.* Independent contractors typically serve a number of customers and must try to please all of those customers. That may result in conflicting priorities for the contractor, causing the level of services to vary.

Common types of services that insurers outsource include marketing, sales, advertising, soliciting applications, inputting applications, mailing to policyholders, billing processes, and claim service. Leasing computer hardware is a common means to outsource the risk of obsolescence and its accompanying financial risk. System software is also commonly outsourced, as are maintenance service and some data processing operations, such as file backup.

Vendors and Vendor Systems

Insurers that pioneered electronic data storage and retrieval methods typically had to select from a limited range of hardware options and to hire programmers to create original software. Although vendors have offered information management tools for many years, the PC-based system environment offers considerably greater flexibility to access vendor products and services. Vendors can be contractors seeking to sell their services, in which case they would be providers of outsourced service. They can also be marketers selling or leasing equipment such as computer hardware or software. Many insurers choose leasing, as opposed to ownership, for products that have a high probability of becoming obsolete or that require a high degree of specialized maintenance. Leases for computer equipment and software typically acknowledge the rapidly changing nature of technology by offering lessees the option of upgrading equipment and software when existing equipment and software become significantly obsolete.

Whatever product or service a vendor is to provide, the purchaser or lessee must evaluate the capability and performance of the vendor carefully. Although most vendors that have been in business for several years are highly competent and consistently try to satisfy their customers, vendor quality can change and not all vendors have equal capability. The following are vendor characteristics that should be considered regardless of the product or service being considered:

- Financial stability—how long the vendor has been in business, historical profitability, financial resources, organizational status as a subsidiary, parent corporation financial status, stability, and corporate philosophy
- Maturity of product—whether the vendor provides all of the products or services needed or whether the vendor depends on other providers for some components, whether the products are well tested in real applications, how much knowledge is required to operate the product, and what the vendor's experience with product introduction, employee training, and integration with existing systems has been
- Vendor staff capability—whether vendor staff members are experienced, stable, and competent in installing and servicing the product, whether they are familiar with unique insurance environment needs, and to what extent they will be available after the product has been delivered or installed
- Customer experience and satisfaction—whether the vendor's existing customers are satisfied with the vendor's product or service

The process of selecting vendor products or services affecting access to data requires the following:

- Analysis of system capabilities and limitations
- Examination of references from current users
- Decisions on which system best meets the organization's needs
- Negotiation for needed components and services to be well-defined in a formal agreement

Installing the System

After selecting a system and reaching agreement with the provider, the insurer must develop an implementation plan. Most insurers, brokers, and agencies have been using electronic systems for many years. Changes in technology are likely to require continuous updates to information systems. Some of those updates will be performed automatically by downloading software revisions to user networks or by temporarily accessing network programs that do not reside in the long-term storage of the user's computer. Computer hardware will probably need periodic updating, maintenance, and, in some cases, complete replacement. Consequently, the quality of the equipment's delivery, set up, and maintenance is an important part of any vendor agreement. When changes to systems are made, vendors participate to differing degrees in designing and carrying out the implementation process. The specific participation should be clearly defined in the vendor lease or purchase agreement. The following items should be considered in defining the implementation plan:

- *Site and workstation preparation.* Are any hard-wiring or space reconfigurations required?
- *Forms and supplies required.* Do system changes necessitate revision to input forms, laser print functions, or preprinted forms (for example, storage or assembly of policies or endorsements)?
- *Equipment location and set up.* Are any significant changes to employee locations, hardware installations, workstations, or work flow implicated?
- *Systems testing.* How thoroughly has the system been tested in similar environments? How thoroughly will it be tested in the purchaser's/lessee's environment before it is active? How long will parallel systems be operated?
- *Removal and redemption of obsolete equipment.* If equipment is being replaced because of upgrades or obsolescence, what responsibilities will the vendor assume for liquidation, and what costs will be involved?

- *Training of users.* Will the vendor participate in creating structured training, setting training objectives, selecting training methods, and providing trainers?

- *Conversion of existing data.* Are losses of access to data likely when data stored in one format are modified for a new system? How much time will the conversion process require, and what are the resource implications?

Most of the data that insurers require to underwrite and issue insurance policies are collected, recorded, and processed as electronic information. Outsourcing electronic information needs can offer potential advantages for some organizations, but care must be exercised in selecting vendors.

Summary

Many of the jobs being created in the United States are in the information or knowledge business and require employees who can access, interpret, and communicate information. Property and liability insurance organizations are entities that generate knowledge or information products rather than manufactured goods. As customers increasingly expect prompt decisions and fast service from insurance knowledge workers, management must grant greater authority to those employees.

Information technology played a major role in the 1980s in motivating organizations to reexamine their work processing procedures. PC-based systems increased the number of processes that could be performed electronically and expanded the availability of information to any employee with a PC. The greater access to data simultaneously improved service and raised customer and regulator expectations for prompt insurer responses. By the 1990s, efficient operation and quality service had become requirements rather than added values. This new business environment requires employees who can use data efficiently.

The following framework helps structure the evaluation of an insurer's information management needs:

- Identifying needed data and sources
- Converting data to information
- Deciding who can best use information
- Assessing costs
- Verifying accuracy and consistency of data

Insurers set objectives at three levels: strategic (long term), tactical (short term), and operational (process oriented). An insurer's objectives influence its data and information needs. Three broad categories of information needs closely correspond to the three categories of organizational objectives: unstructured (strategic), semistructured (tactical), and structured (operational). Because performance objectives are also set at strategic, tactical, and operational levels, insurers establish methods to monitor performance accordingly. Individual employees use data and information to set personal objectives, measure their performance, and accomplish their own career objectives.

The two primary categories of electronic systems for recording data and accessing information are mainframe-based systems and PC-based systems. Mainframe computers are particularly useful for statistical record keeping, financial analysis, and results comparisons over several years. PCs permit insurers to send and receive many items of data simultaneously in files. Problems occur when modern systems depend on data coded for and stored in older legacy systems. PC-based approaches to organizing data can help to overcome those problems.

Insurers that are displeased with their current information systems must weigh the costs and benefits of adopting a new system. Insurers can also outsource their information systems needs, but they must evaluate vendors carefully.

The next chapter provides examples of how information is analyzed to identify policy production, underwriting, and claim processes.

Chapter Notes

1. Zenas Block and Ian McMillan, *Corporate Venturing: Creating New Business Within the Firm* (Boston, MA: Harvard Business School Press, 1995), p. 2.
2. Michael Hammer and James Champy, *Reengineering the Corporation* (New York, NY: Harper & Bros., 1993), p. 24.
3. Hammer and Champy, p. 25.

Chapter 3

Using Information Resources

Insurers need access to data for information that affects the primary functions of marketing, underwriting, and claim handling. This chapter reviews some of a typical insurer's specific data needs for these functions and describes how security concerns and organizational philosophies affect the information systems of insurers.

Marketing Information

Insurers, like most businesses, seek growth in revenue. Revenue for insurers is derived primarily from insurance premiums. Growth is especially important to insurers because the cost of losses increases over time, and the rate of that increase can be greater than the rate at which earned premiums increase. Incurred losses increase because of increasing medical and legal costs associated with settling liability claims and because of increasing costs to repair and replace damaged property. Rate increases offset most of the rising claim costs, but competition from other insurers and regulatory restrictions on rate levels often prevent insurers from increasing operating profits with rate increases. Also, regulators are reluctant to approve rate increases that contain significant expense components such as those associated with new computer systems, more extensive administrative services, or higher acquisition costs like those resulting from commission and other sales incentives. Consequently, increases in operating profits depend on the insurer's ability to increase the number of policies it writes while controlling the incurred losses as much as possible and limiting underwriting expenses.

An example helps to explain the need for growth in premium from sources other than rate increases. Suppose hypothetical Big Regional Stock Insurance Company (BRSIC) has been marketing personal auto and homeowners insurance through independent insurance agents in Ohio, Indiana, Illinois, and Missouri for over fifty years. BRSIC once had over 300 agents selling its products, but many agents have merged their businesses, forming larger agencies, or have retired and sold their businesses. BRSIC now has only 150 agents, but the company's policy count has remained stable, and rate increases have kept pace with rising claims. BRSIC has reduced expenses whenever possible and limited its investment in computers and other equipment. Consequently, BRSIC has been consistently profitable, producing an average of 8 percent in investment income and 2 percent in underwriting profits.

BRSIC's board of directors believes that BRSIC is too conservative in its marketing strategy. The premium to surplus ratio is 1.5 to 1, which means the company has ample capital with which to grow if it could find a way to increase sales without jeopardizing profit. In a recent board meeting, the chairman of the board, Jones, challenged BRSIC's president, Smith, to explain why the company was not growing. Smith explained that aggressive competition and the decreasing number of agents have limited growth in the four states where BRSIC operates. Jones and the board of directors believe that the company's $200 million in surplus should be producing greater profits than the 10 percent level it has been producing. Jones and the board have now demanded that Smith identify new products, new territories, new distribution methods, or some other method of increasing premium volume by the next quarterly board meeting.

This scenario is not unusual. Investors and owners have become accustomed to relatively high profits with the success of the stock market. In the last decade of the twentieth century, annual investment returns were frequently 10 percent or more. Consequently, insurer owners, anticipating underwriting profits of at least 5 percent, are likely to demand insurer operating profits of at least 15 percent (10 percent from investments and 5 percent from underwriting). Insurer management must respond to owner expectations for reasonable profits or risk the possibility that owners will reduce their investments (by selling their stock) or will change management. The ability to access data and organize the data into useful information is crucially important in planning insurer growth, as illustrated by the continuing example of BRSIC.

BRSIC President Smith considers the options Jones suggested for growth: new products, new territories, new distribution methods, and other methods of increasing premium volume. To decide which of these might best help BRSIC grow, Smith needs data and information.

Products

Before considering additional products that might be sold, Smith reviews the current products and how well they seem to be meeting customer expectations. Smith called his marketing vice president, Abel, and underwriting officer, Careful, and arranged a meeting in which they reviewed data sources from which information has been identified (see Exhibit 3-1).

Information developed from analyzing the data sources suggests that although BRSIC has a good reputation with its customers, the customers tend to be older than the customers of most other insurers and that the average age of BRSIC's customers is rising. Younger drivers seem to be choosing competitors for their insurance (or the average age of residents in BRSIC's territories is rising). Rate increases and expense controls have offset rising losses. However, after expenses reach their lowest likely percentage, the combined ratio for personal auto will probably begin to rise.

The auto information suggests that some profitability problems are developing, but the homeowners information appears favorable. Both loss and expense ratios are decreasing, and the competitive position suggests that BRSIC has a marketing advantage for price among higher-valued residences. Employee retention is better than average. Although that retention might improve stability, long-term employees may be less likely than new employees to identify product or service innovations that could increase growth.

The following discussion suggests how BRSIC might use the data analysis to develop a growth plan based on products. A quick review of this information suggests that, in choosing among existing products, Smith might improve profits more readily if growth plans emphasized homeowners insurance rather than auto insurance. The highly competitive nature of BRSIC's rates for higher-valued homes suggests a possible market niche. An auto rate increase would improve the loss ratio and simultaneously increase premium. BRSIC might also investigate why younger operators represent a declining percentage of its personal auto customers. The information about the average insured driver's age being lower than BRSIC's average may suggest that BRSIC is unnecessarily restricting eligibility among younger operators. If some segment of the younger operators with better-than-average loss experience could be identified (such as married operators over age nineteen), underwriting eligibility might be justified. A product change (a coverage or pricing modification, perhaps) might increase appeal to a desirable younger market segment. Many of BRSIC's auto insurance customers do not insure their homes with BRSIC, so product opportunities might exist to sell homeowners coverage to auto customers.

Exhibit 3-1
Available Data Sources and Information

Data source	Information
A recent summary of 2,000 customer satisfaction surveys	BRSIC has a good reputation for prompt and fair service for both auto and homeowners.
An auto insurance customer profile report; industry data	The average age of BRSIC's insured drivers is significantly higher than the industry average in each of the four states in which it writes business.
Homeowners insurance customer profile report; industry data	The average value of BRSIC's insured homes is significantly higher than the industry average.
A comparison of the most recent auto profile report with similar reports for the previous five years	The average age of drivers is increasing.
Auto loss and expense ratio reports over five years	The auto loss ratio has been increasing slightly, but the expense ratio has been decreasing sufficiently to offset the rising loss ratio.
Homeowners loss and expense ratio reports	BRSIC has been profitable (combined ratio below 98 percent), with combined ratio improving over five years.
Human resource profile reports	The typical employee has been employed by BRSIC for an average of ten years, which is a significantly higher rate of employee retention than for BRSIC's competitors. The same reports indicate BRSIC's salary levels are similar to the levels of other similar local employees.
An industry rate comparison for personal auto and homeowners	BRSIC's personal auto rates are average among twenty leading competitors; BRSIC's homeowners rates are average for lower-valued homes and very competitive for homes valued $150,000 and above.
A comparison of insureds with auto coverage and insureds with homeowners coverage	Most auto insurance customers do not have their homes insured with BRSIC.

Besides enhancements to existing products, BRSIC might also consider offering additional products. Since BRSIC has producers and employees who are experienced and competent in handling personal auto and homeowners insurance, it would probably limit its new product considerations to similar types of products. However, those might include coverage for personal boats, campers, recreational vehicles, excess personal liability, personal effects, personal computer coverage, or any other related coverage that BRSIC has apparently chosen not to offer. BRSIC might consider creating new products and services targeted for the needs of customers who own higher-valued homes, given its competitive homeowners pricing position for such customers.

Before initiating an aggressive marketing plan to increase premium by selling new products, an insurer must assess the potential for profit. In the case of selling to owners of higher-valued homes, BRSIC might isolate premium and loss data for insured homeowners with residence coverage limits (Coverage A) over $150,000 to verify whether underwriting profits have been satisfactory for products already being sold to those insureds. Sometimes such analyses reveal that products with the most competitive rates are only marginally profitable and are often subsidized by products that are less competitive in the market. Should data analysis reveal that to be the case, new products or services designed for the higher-valued home market could be priced to help offset perceived inadequacies in the homeowners rate for that market segment.

Telephone surveys are conducted by asking a predetermined group a limited number of structured questions, the answers to which are recorded and analyzed.

Once BRSIC decides on a possible course of product action, it might seek additional information from its producers or customers. A **telephone survey** of customers would be one way to quickly sample opinion. **Focus groups** of producers could be assembled over lunch to discuss the likely success of several alternatives. Data from surveys and focus groups, combined with the information previously described, would help Smith choose growth alternatives for presentation at the next board meeting.

Focus groups are small groups of customers or potential customers brought together to provide opinions about a specific product service or need, or another issue.

Territories

Changes in territory also require data and information. Some of the data sources and information Smith might require are shown in Exhibit 3-2.

Exhibit 3-2
Data Source and Information Needs

Data source	Information
A recent comparison of industry results for the four states in which BRSIC operates	Loss ratios for both auto and homeowners are best for the industry in Ohio, next best in Missouri, and less profitable in the other two states.
Past analysis of industry competitiveness by state	Competition is traditionally most aggressive in Ohio for all personal lines but only average in Missouri.
State rate level analysis among leading personal lines insurers	BRSIC's products are most competitively priced in Missouri.
BRSIC's state level premium and loss reports	Missouri is the most profitable state among the four states in which BRSIC sells coverage for personal auto and homeowners.
Reports showing BRSIC's distribution of premium by geographic territory (urban, suburban, and rural) in all four states; industry data	BRSIC has a greater than industry average percentage of rural and suburban risks.
State economic statistics	Rural populations are declining, and urban and suburban populations are increasing.
BRSIC's five-year loss and expense ratios	BRSIC's ratios are lowest in rural territories.
BRSIC's rates for auto and homeowners compared with competitors'	BRSIC's rates are most competitive in rural territories.

From this information, Smith, Able, and Careful determine that although industry profitability is greatest in Ohio, the lower level of competition in Missouri, combined with its history of being a profitable state for BRSIC, makes it the most attractive state for increased marketing emphasis. The company's results seem to support continuing its competitive position in rural and suburban locations, even though rural populations are declining. BRSIC might consider alternatives for increasing market share in rural and suburban territories.

In addition to reviewing data and information about existing territories, Smith might seek information about additional territories, particularly those in contiguous states. If BRSIC has marketers, underwriting, and claim personnel who are familiar with neighboring Kentucky and Illinois, for example, and if an analysis of data from those states reveals they are as attractive as Missouri, Smith might gather additional data and information about marketing opportunities in either or both of those states. Similarly, since BRSIC has traditionally emphasized rural and suburban marketing territories, it might identify new marketing opportunities in urban communities. In some states, insurers are required to offer coverage in cities. By voluntarily identifying desirable urban markets, BRSIC might achieve compliance with such regulations while preserving profitability objectives.

Distribution Methods

Technological improvements in data storage and access permit the rapid review of information, as discussed in the BRSIC example. Insurers access data from their own proprietary sources (premium, losses, and expenses) and from a wide range of externally available data sources. Those external data sources permit insurers and other businesses to organize, or segment, prospective customers into homogeneous groups. Such segmentation facilitates matching product design and distribution method with anticipated needs of specific customer groups. Data that better define the nature of particular homogeneous groups help insurers choose the most appropriate distribution method.

Customers

Credit card companies are an example of organizations that collect extensive customer data. Credit card companies use information from credit report data to qualify prospective customers for different levels of credit. They can also sort their customers according to seasonal spending patterns, types of purchases, average monthly charges, payment size and frequency, income ranges, and other demographic characteristics. Given the detailed data available to credit card companies, many can assemble a data subset of all cardholders who match a defined set of characteristics.

Suppose, based on its analysis of the previous information, that BRSIC decides to sell more homeowners insurance policies to owners of high-valued homes located in suburban communities in western Kentucky. To obtain extensive data about prospective customers, BRSIC could contract with an aggressive credit card company to identify members of alumni associations with a minimum annual household income of perhaps $70,000 who spend at least $200 a month on credit card purchases and who always pay their bills on time. Further suppose that BRSIC obtains computerized listings from real estate transactions (public records) that identify homes that sold for more than $150,000 but less than $500,000 within the past five years. Combining this data with the credit card company's data, BRSIC should be able to identify a group of potential customers for competitively priced homeowners policies in western Kentucky.

Suppose that BRSIC performs a telephone customer survey among a representative group from the targeted prospective customers and gathers data revealing that most of those households own personal computers connected to the Internet. Using a name search program for Internet addresses, BRSIC might begin a marketing campaign using Internet or e-mail communication for each name on the credit card company's list of prospective customers. BRSIC might offer the resulting list of Internet users a free service, such as homeowners replacement cost analysis or contents valuation, and then solicit homeowners sales or other products and services that BRSIC believes the **target group** would value.

> A **target group** is a collection of individuals who have been identified as desirable customers.

BRSIC might prefer not to market to customers directly through the Internet. It might prefer to arrange an Internet marketing strategy in cooperation with a producer who has already established a network of personal insurance customers.

Besides Internet options, BRSIC could arrange a joint venture with a credit card company or bank to market insurance products using the financial institution's billing process and customer service facilities. BRSIC could pay a handling fee to the financial institution for its marketing services much the way it pays a commission to a traditional agent.

This discussion is not intended to provide a comprehensive analysis of insurer marketing options, nor is it intended to recommend one method of insurance marketing over others. Insurers and other financial institutions will likely use multiple methods to reach customers and will be limited only by their imaginations and regulatory constraints. However, access to data and the ability to manipulate it into useful information are crucial for an organization's evolving growth strategy. Senior managers from aggressive insurance organizations are unlikely to need pressure from shareholders and owners to begin identifying new growth opportunities. Aggressive organizations identify new data sources that help them lead the industry in new marketing strategies.

Underwriting Information

In 1960, most insurance underwriting was performed manually. Producers completed paper applications for insurance coverage, consulted books and manuals to calculate rates, performed computations by hand, and often collected premiums in cash. Insurers received paper applications and assigned clerks to refer them to appropriate examiners, who identified missing information and then contacted producers to obtain the missing components. Complete, or nearly complete, applications were then passed to the first level of underwriting authority for review of pricing and risk characteristic acceptability. Applications were referred to different levels of underwriting authority until someone ultimately decided to accept or reject the risk, and, if to accept, at what price.

Also part of that process was decision making about whether additional investigative information would be necessary (for example, loss control reports, claim histories, inspections, credit reports, and motor vehicle reports). When additional information was needed, someone was assigned to request the information and follow up to verify that it was received and appropriately evaluated. Given that lengthy and manually intensive process, customers and producers frequently waited weeks for insurers to make decisions.

For insurance professionals who work for progressive insurance organizations and who began their insurance careers after 1980, that process seems antiquated. The progressive insurer of the 1990s accepts applications from producers and insureds electronically, using computer devices that were not common even in 1980, let alone 1960. Today, the producer or customer service representative (CSR) knows whether the application is complete as it is entered on a personal computer (PC) because the computer can verify that needed information is provided. Electronic applications are often automatically screened by a computer program, accepted if meeting insurer guidelines, or referred to underwriters for further evaluation. If referred, the information is transmitted immediately to someone with sufficient authority to determine price and acceptability. Once deemed acceptable (or rejected), policy forms and coverage documentation (or cancellation notices) are processed by a system that establishes premium accounting, statistical records, billing processes, commission payments, inspection and report ordering, follow-up action, and a record of coverage for claim processing.

Personal Lines

Insurers have paid much attention to data collection and information sorting for personal lines underwriting since 1980. Part of that attention was motivated by competitive pressure from consumers seeking the lowest possible price. Insurer use of electronic data access and information has reduced the need for manual handling, resulting in savings in jobs and salaries. Those savings mitigate the cost of the insurance product, which is ultimately reflected in the premiums consumers pay.

Personal insurance products, especially personal auto liability coverages, tend to be more publicly visible than commercial insurance products. Regulators require highly detailed premium, loss, and expense reports and expect personal lines insurers to be particularly sensitive in monitoring customer complaints. Personal lines insurers have found that highly detailed data collection and analysis are typically required to justify rate changes, particularly for personal auto liability insurance. In addition, the public sensitivity to rising auto insurance rates has motivated politicians, regulators, and insurers to collect and analyze data at very refined levels.

Another reason personal lines insurers have tended to lead commercial insurers in the use of data and information management is that data about individuals, relevant to insurance purchasing decisions, have long been available electronically. Motor vehicle operator reports, past accident and claim history, and credit reports are examples of available data that personal lines insurers have used for many years.

Finally, because the profiles of most personal insurance risks are relatively similar within homogeneous groups, personal lines insurers tend to emphasize the evaluation of groups, or portfolios of risks, rather than concentrating on evaluating individual policies, as is often the case with commercial lines policies. Since many commercial policies involve large numbers of exposures (multiple properties, products, or employees) and potentially more frequent and larger losses and because they generate premiums that are higher, on average, than most personal insurance policies, the practice of closely evaluating individual commercial policies may be warranted. The tendency of personal lines insurers to evaluate portfolios of risks might encourage them to make greater use of collections of data for evaluating their results and planning objectives.

Commercial Lines

Commercial insurers increasingly depend on collecting and evaluating large sets of data, much as personal lines insurers have been doing for years. Workers compensation is one line of insurance that benefits from the availability of comprehensive data. Coverage and rates for workers compensation are typically defined by state statute, as are premium discounts and credits. Policy premiums usually depend on the number of employees, the salaries paid, the type of work performed (and its statistical likelihood of generating injuries), and the number and cost of claims the employer experiences over different time periods. Consequently, individual insurers have difficulty differentiating their products using coverage or rates.

Insurers sometimes use their underwriting and loss control services to differentiate themselves from competitors. Insurers collect data that employers can use to better understand the causes of their losses. Insurers also use data to define recommendations that can reduce future losses and improve claim frequency and severity. Data that effectively identify employees who seem susceptible to certain types of injuries can help the employer consider possible employee reassignments. From an analysis of claim data, insurers can also identify specific job activities that generate frequent injuries. Employers can use that information to modify job functions and procedures, which can reduce the probability that injuries will occur.

Reduction of the frequency and severity of employee injuries both helps maintain higher employee productivity and lowers workers compensation insurance costs, which should contribute to greater profitability for the insured's business. The accuracy of insurer data for the number of employees, the salaries paid, the type of work performed or job classification (which reflects statistical likelihood of generating injuries), and the number and cost of claims is crucial for determining the correct premium.

Sources of that data include employer payroll records, insurer premium audits, prior insurance policies, prior insurance rates, insurance claim frequency and severity histories, injury reports to state workers compensation authorities, the average claim frequency and severity for similar businesses, and the average numbers of employees in each major classification for similar businesses. All of these sources must be compared to identify any inconsistencies among the sources. Computer programs that can compare such data as number of employees in each classification with the total gross sales can help in identifying inconsistencies. Underwriters try to verify that the employee job classifications accurately reflect the actual activities of the employees and that payroll amounts assigned to each classification realistically reflect the numbers of employees performing the work.

Obtaining accurate rating data for workers compensation insurance can sometimes be difficult because the initial premium for each policy period is based on the insured's estimate of probable employee classifications and payroll amounts for the next twelve months. Insurers that fail to identify changes in payroll base their premium on data that may have changed significantly from the estimate. Insureds have difficulty accurately forecasting their employment needs. Furthermore, since their initial premium is based on an estimate of payroll, insureds have an incentive (a lower initial premium payment) to underestimate payroll, numbers of employees, or classifications of higher rated jobs.

The Importance of Accurate Data

Contractor is insured with Insurer. Contractor assumes that only 50 percent of the jobs quoted in a given year actually result in contracts to perform work. Consequently, Contractor estimates payroll based on 50 percent of the possible work that could be received over the coming year. If 70 percent of Contractor's contracts are actually accepted, the amount of payroll could be considerably higher than Contractor's estimates. If, in addition to underestimating the number of jobs and revenue, Contractor failed to include in the payroll estimate the wages of a significant number of high-exposure jobs, Insurer would have based its initial premium on data that reflected less than actual loss exposure.

To ensure that adequate rates are charged, insurers perform premium audits to collect data about changes in employee classification and payroll distributions. Premium audits also quantify data showing numbers of employees and changing distribution of work among large or small projects. In addition, insurers perform loss control inspections to collect data about how well the work being performed matches the employee classifications being used to determine the premium.

Similar data are also collected in lines of insurance other than workers compensation. Commercial auto underwriters are interested in periodically assessing such data as driver violation and accident records, driver safety training programs, vehicle maintenance logs, vehicle mileage, vehicle condition, driver lists (to identify new drivers, driver experience, and turnover), changes in routes driven, types of freight hauled, claim records, and many other items. Information systems can be designed to identify potential areas of concern among these types of data, producing reports that summarize data so that underwriters can assess the level of exposure, available coverage limits, rates, credits, and surcharges. Without information systems, underwriters must evaluate the data elements individually to assess the overall exposure. As with employee classifications and payroll distribution for workers compensation, the cost to assess the commercial auto exposure justifies the cost of obtaining and interpreting the data in most cases. Some data, such as detailed assessments of employee physical condition and medical history for workers compensation insurance, are either too costly to obtain for routine underwriting purposes or are unavailable.

The Importance of Accurate Data

Trucker reports to Insurer on an annual survey form that none of its drivers have had any convictions for driving violations in the past three years. Although Trucker might believe that statement to be true, underwriters usually obtain individual motor vehicle operator histories at least annually for most commercial auto customers. Similarly, Trucker might report that its own mechanics perform both routine and comprehensive vehicle service, recording all work in a log. That might also be true at a point in time, but the loss of a key mechanic or another employee might interrupt the performance of safety-related repairs that could indirectly lead to a loss. Data should be updated periodically.

Periodic inspections by loss control representatives are one means by which underwriters gather new data to assess the accuracy of existing data on which rates are based. Inspections of commercial property risks are also important for collecting data about the values exposed to loss, changes in the use of the property, building contents, and liability exposures from injuries that can occur on the property. Contractors and businesses that perform services for others also incur obligations to protect those for whom they perform work. For example, a building owner might require a contractor that installs signs over public sidewalks to assume liability for claims brought against the owner as a result of injuries that occur to pedestrians because of a sign. Data describing the nature of those contractual obligations must also be assessed periodically to quantify exposure and to verify their consistency with the services for which the insurer's rates were established.

Similarly, insurers must periodically evaluate the income or sales revenue received by insured commercial entities to verify that the magnitude of commercial activity is consistent with the sales revenue anticipated when the underwriters' rates were established. Of particular importance to insurers that provide products liability coverages is careful assessment of consumer exposures created by manufactured products. Loss control and premium audit specialists gather important data for these information needs, but reports assessing industry loss trends and developing exposures that characterize a particular category of businesses are other important sources of data. A large volume of data is needed to assess the loss exposures of large and specialized commercial entities adequately. Because extensive data analysis is needed to develop useful information for risk selection and pricing, underwriters responsible for complex insureds tend to develop expertise in a few categories of businesses.

Claim Information

Rapid access to accurate data is essential for effective claim handling. Customers increasingly demand coverage answers immediately when reporting a loss. Fortunately, modern interactive databases are available to claim professionals much the way they are available to those who work in underwriting and marketing.

Collecting Loss Data, Determining Coverage, and Referring Assignments

Claim CSRs receive loss reports by telephone (also by fax, e-mail, or Internet communication) sometimes from producers but often directly from insureds and claimants. (Sometimes CSRs also perform sales, underwriting, and processing functions.) Most insurers have computer systems that permit CSRs to inquire of the database whether a particular caller is covered and, if so, with what coverage and limits. Underwriting records that reveal applicable policy forms and endorsements are readily accessible, as are lists of insured locations, individuals, policy periods, and details of changes made during policy periods. Prior claim records help CSRs identify duplicate reports of the same loss (occurring when multiple claimants or insureds report claims from the same occurrence).

Computer prompts appear on CSR monitors to help them identify needed data to establish the insurer's claim record. The collection of that data permits the system and the CSR to determine whether the details of the claim appear to match the coverage provided by the policies affected. When the date input by the CSR does not clearly match the applicable dates of coverage, the system can provide suggested responses for the CSR and direct the CSR as to how best to refer the claim.

Suppose Company G insures Warehouse for loss from fire. Without an interactive system that can make coverage data immediately available, Company G would need to locate a paper file describing Warehouse's insurance coverage before it could respond to a claim. If a paper file is being reviewed for underwriting, billing, or some other reason, the CSR might need to search for that file on multiple desks and in multiple file cabinets. If claim representatives are using the file to update data concerning another claim, the desks and the file cabinets of claim professionals might also need to be searched. Sometimes when paper files cannot be found, producers (and insureds) are asked for copies of declarations pages, endorsements, or insurance applications to verify coverage.

If Company G does not have a fax machine or other electronic means to transport evidence of coverage rapidly, the CSR might need to wait several days before receiving confirmation of coverage details. Since many insurers use electronic communication to speed service to customers and since many customers are aware of the rapid service capabilities electronic networks make possible, customer service expectations are higher today than ever before. Consequently, customers often perceive service delays resulting from using mail or slow electronics as unnecessary and unreasonable. Perceived service delays cause customer and claimant disappointment and sometimes anger. Disappointed and angry insureds often expect higher claim settlements than they would if their claim was handled more efficiently. Disappointed and angry customers and claimants might also complain to insurance regulators. That can result in regulator inquiries about claim-handling procedures and possibly fines for inappropriate claim-handling practices.

Alternatively, suppose Company G has electronic access to coverage data and a Warehouse officer calls the company's CSR to report a fire in the loading dock area of a 20,000-square foot building. The CSR receiving the call can immediately check the computer data file to see whether the insurer provides coverage for the customer and for the building involved. If coverage might be available, the CSR, aided by prompts incorporated within the claim input screens, begins asking Warehouse's officer a series of questions intended to help the CSR determine the likelihood of coverage. The officer's responses are input into the claim reporting system as the CSR asks the questions. If the circumstances of the loss, as defined by the data collected and input by the CSR, match a set of criteria programmed into the input edits of the computer system, the system might advise the CSR about how to proceed. If coverage appears likely and the loss involves a small amount of property damage, the CSR might tell the insured to obtain an estimate of repairs and fax it to the insurer. If the loss is large or involves liability to others, the system might determine which claim representative (depending on experience and authority level required to deal with the loss) will be assigned to investigate the claim. The CSR might give the name and phone number of that claim representative to the Warehouse officer. The customer, in this case an officer of the insured organization, having heard from the CSR that a coverage record exists and that a specific person has been assigned to investigate, is likely to be more satisfied than would have been the case had the processing been done manually.

Many insurers insist that their claim representatives contact claimants and insureds within twelve hours after the customer or claimant reports the loss. If Insurer G can collect and access data, verify coverage, and assign the claim investigation quickly, it can probably also electronically advise a particular claim representative of the assignment of each loss, either through the insurer's e-mail system or by some other method of electronic communication. Some systems can also send messages to claim representatives by cellular transmission to a phone or pager. Consequently, claim representatives can be assigned responsibility to investigate a claim and notified of that assignment as they are traveling or investigating other losses. By using cellular phones, claim representatives can contact insureds and claim representatives within minutes of the report of a loss to a CSR.

Although such rapid claim handling might not be required when the amount of loss is small, such as a car windshield damaged by a stone, it can be instrumental in limiting the magnitude of loss in claims involving bodily injury and large amounts of property damage. A highly competent claim representative who contacts an injured claimant within hours of a loss report has a greater opportunity to gain the claimant's confidence (that the claim will be treated promptly and fairly) than a claim representative who does not make contact for several days. Prompt contact permits the claim representative to evaluate whether injured claimants have received appropriate medical attention and to identify and help arrange property repairs if necessary. Such prompt and appropriate claim handling frequently results in a lower cost of indemnification and a lower settlement amount than for losses that are settled more slowly. Furthermore, greater claimant confidence in the claim representative might reduce the likelihood of the claimant choosing to hire an attorney, which can inflate loss amounts and delay settlement. The availability of customer coverage and loss data, analyzed quickly and accurately to verify coverage, combined with claim personnel's ability to communicate effectively and rapidly, can help an insurer establish a reputation for effective claim handling and minimize unnecessary costs.

Using Data To Distinguish Claim Service

Although improving claim service and reducing costs are important, an insurer's data collection and information processing capacity can be used to distinguish the insurer for its unique service. The senior manager of one insurer reviewed its data collection and electronic communication system capabilities and concluded that claim representatives should be able to establish customer contact within twenty minutes of the first report of loss. Accustomed to an industry in which customer contact within twenty-four hours is considered the standard, many of this insurer's claim representatives doubted that average contact time could be reduced to as little as twenty minutes. However, because of the availability of technology that gathers data, performs comparisons, and quickly makes assignments to appropriate individuals and because of this company's excellent detail of claim service records, efforts to achieve a twenty-minute average response time have resulted in most claimants being contacted within two hours, perhaps the fastest claim service available from any insurer.

Whether that level of service is necessary depends on the customer's expectation and the circumstances of the loss. For the repair of a minor dent in an auto fender, many customers may not care whether they receive a call from their insurer within two hours or a day. However, desperate homeowners who cannot live in their home as a result of major damage from a windstorm have different expectations. An insurer that can deliver a check for costs associated with additional living expenses within hours of the claim report might be perceived as delivering outstanding service. Such service might be especially important if a catastrophic loss resulted in damage to many homes in a limited geographic area. An insurer could distinguish itself by establishing a neighborhood claim service office in a motor home, from which it might dispatch claim representatives with authority to make immediate settlements, using portable battery-operated computers and cellular phone connections to access insurer coverage data. Similar mobile service facilities can be installed in minivans, which can be used instead of the sedans traditionally used as transportation for claim representatives. Claimant and witness statements can be taken inside the van, which can double as the claim representative's office and communication center. It might contain the following equipment:

- Portable battery-operated laptop computers
- Cellular telephone connection for voice and digital transmission
- Portable fax machines
- Portable printers with check-producing capability
- Digital cameras to record and transmit images
- Satellite transmission and receiving antennae
- Television and radio receiving equipment
- Videotape, audiotape, and digital recording and playback machines

- VHF and other broadcast transceivers
- Alternating current (AC) electric power generators
- Digital and manual repair service and material directories

Such equipment, easily installed in a conventional minivan, provides mobile claim representatives significantly greater access to data and information than most permanent insurer regional claim offices possessed in the 1980s. If an insurer had a large market share in a major metropolitan area, it might justify the expense of assigning a few of these vans for the purpose of taking the claim office to the loss location within minutes of the loss report.

With the increasing popularity of cellular phones in automobiles, a motorist involved in an accident could use a cellular phone to report the accident to an insurer. The call could be directed by cellular connection to a mobile office where a claim representative could record the loss description while driving to the accident location. The on-board computer could simultaneously be accessing the customer's coverage record and determining coverage availability. The claim representative could arrive at the accident scene while emergency vehicles are still at the site. Payment of the claim could occur at the scene of the accident. Customers are likely to perceive such service as superior to any service not equally efficient. As insurers develop improved access to data, insurance professionals capable of interpreting the data for coverage information and determination of settlement amounts will define new standards for claim handling.

Virtual Claim Offices

Technology will likely permit insurers to develop virtual claim offices. To aid in settling losses from automobile accidents, digital cameras with digital wireless communication capability (which already exist) could become standard equipment aboard police vehicles. Police reports might include a detailed camera inspection of an accident scene. A computer chip identifying which insurer provides insurance coverage might be incorporated in vehicle inspection stickers. (Such a chip could also be incorporated in drivers' licenses or other forms of identification.) The police might use an electronic scanning device to extract detailed information about the insurer and the insured without interacting with the operators of the vehicles. The collected data could be transmitted to police headquarters and copied automatically to the insurers involved. Insurers could interpret the digital images, police narrative description, coverage, vehicle, and customer data while the accident investigation was proceeding. To the degree that coverage can be determined from such sources, a preliminary coverage determination can be made from anywhere electronic connection can be arranged. If the loss is covered, money, or its credit equivalent, can be immediately transferred from the insurer's account to the account of a repair facility indicated as the customer's preference in the computer chip contained in the vehicle registration sticker. The same chip might contain information (gathered and stored with the insured's consent) about preferred medical treatment facilities, health and life insurance, closest relatives, employment, legal service, whether the insured is an organ donor, and other relevant information. Should such a comprehensive accident reporting system become available, a police report could become the primary data source for claim settlements.

Automatic Reserving

Insurers have long collected data describing the amounts of their paid losses. They typically categorize such data by line of business, coverage, territory, state, injury type, cause of injury, calendar year, and accident year. When a loss is reported, insurers estimate an amount likely to settle each claim. The estimated amounts are called **case reserves**.

A **case reserve** is the amount of money claim representatives estimate will be needed to settle a claim.

Experienced claim representatives who have handled hundreds of similar claims can usually estimate the amount needed to settle a particular claim. For example, claim representatives who specialize in settling losses involving damages to buildings are familiar with local material, architectural, and other construction costs and can usually accurately assess the amounts needed to settle a claim.

Unfortunately, case reserves for liability losses are more difficult to estimate, even for experienced claim representatives. Liability losses frequently involve bodily injuries for which future medical treatment may be difficult to forecast accurately.

Another factor complicating case reserves for liability claims is that many involve claimants represented by attorneys. Liability claims often involve bodily injuries that result in permanent disability, disfigurement, or other reduced physical or mental capacity. The dollar value of indemnification for reduced capacity varies considerably depending on the extent of the injury, the pre-loss income and performance level of the victim, and the victim's age and expected life span. In addition to these uncertainties, ultimate settlement amounts for liability claims are affected by the volume and believability of the plaintiff's attorney's evidence, the negotiating skill of the plaintiff's attorney, and the way in which the court that presides over a disputed settlement tends to judge the settlement values of tried liability claims.

Insurers that can review, during their initial assessment of a claim, a large number of similar past claims can better use their experience to set case reserves accurately. Because of their familiarity with large numbers of claims, experienced claim representatives and field managers can be instrumental in helping an insurer establish accurate case reserves.

Accurate case reserves are important to insurers because they are treated, for insurance accounting purposes, as incurred losses. An insurer's financial records are immediately adjusted for the liability created by incurred losses because a case reserve is a liability for an amount owed to a claimant that will be paid when the amount is more accurately quantified and accepted by the claimant.

If, for example, a claim representative receives an assignment to investigate a claimant injury that resulted from an automobile accident, the claim representative, based on his or her experience with similar injuries from auto accidents, might estimate that the claim will be settled for between $30,000 and $50,000. Consequently, a case reserve of $40,000 might be set. The insurer's financial results, which include the total of incurred losses, will immediately reflect the liability for the $40,000 case reserve, even though the final settlement might not occur for two or more years. The subsequent claim investigation might confirm the reasonableness of a $40,000 reserve or develop information that causes the insurer to increase or decrease the reserve amount. The insurer's financial records continue to reflect the liability for the amount of the case reserve and any adjustment subsequently made to the case reserve based on new information until the claim is settled.

As long as the case reserve is reasonably close to the final settlement, this estimating process operates satisfactorily. However, case reserves are only estimates and can be inaccurate. Most insurers make every effort to indemnify claimants for all reasonable medical expenses and lost wages by diligently communicating with accident victims, their families, and medical service providers. However, even well-informed and experienced claim professionals, who have closely monitored the development of a claimant's injuries and have diligently made reasonable payments for indemnification, can be surprised by large claims for accumulated additional medical expenses. Plaintiffs' attorneys frequently accumulate months of charges for medical services and related expenses and submit them immediately before the expiration of a claim's typical two-year statute of limitations. Such claim submissions, if for justifiable expenses, can result in sudden and dramatic changes to case reserves. A sudden large increase in an outstanding case reserve could raise an insurer's incurred losses sufficiently to raise the loss and combined ratios and to lower operating profits.

Because large case reserve adjustments directly affect an insurer's financial results, insurers try to make their initial case reserves and subsequent adjustments as accurate as possible. Although experienced claim professionals contribute significantly to the accuracy of insurer reserves, the availability of electronic data storage and retrieval of past loss experience greatly enhances reserve accuracy. Large numbers of past claim settlements can be sorted rapidly by such characteristics as line of business, coverage, territory, state, injury type, and cause of injury. The information system can synthesize many years of experience by many claim professionals, potentially enhancing the accuracy of case reserves. Electronic data containing highly detailed loss descriptions can be used to sort settlement amounts for particular types of losses according to such loss characteristics as geographic area, court jurisdiction, or attorney representation. By using such detail to inform case reserve decisions, insurers can increase their confidence in setting initial case reserve amounts.

For some losses, especially those that occur with high frequency, electronic information systems can screen the detailed data cells of every new claim description input by a CSR and assign a case reserve based on the averages contained in the database. Claim representatives can then adjust that amount, if necessary, based on their own experience. Insurers have long used minimum or average reserve amounts to establish new case reserves when loss details are limited. However, those minimums and averages are typically set for all of the insurer offices, or at least for large geographic areas. Insurers have begun experimenting with electronic case reserve-setting systems that continually reassess average reserves. Those systems use years of experience adjusted for inflationary effects and other locally variable settlement trends to define case reserves that reflect factors unique to each claim.

Although experienced claim professionals must still monitor such refined automatic reserving capability, some insurers might find that initial case reserves are more accurate when they can rely on an electronic system for part of the reserving process. Reliable estimates of settlement amounts based on large databases are also useful for claim representatives in qualifying the reasonableness of claimant settlement demands. When reasonable settlements are identified quickly, they can lead to prompter claim settlements, faster indemnification for needed medical services and lost wages, increased claimant satisfaction, and fewer complaints, potentially resulting in savings for the insurer.

Besides case reserves, insurers establish reserves for losses that occurred during the year but have not yet been reported (a type of bulk reserve called incurred but not reported, or IBNR) and for anticipated errors in the total of case reserves (broadly categorized as bulk reserves) for each coverage in each line of business. This chapter is not intended to explore insurer claim reserving practices in detail since that is examined in other parts of the CPCU program. However, electronic access to large databases, which improves insurer confidence in case reserving, also raises insurer management's confidence in bulk reserves (typically established by actuarial specialists), which influence insurer financial results.

Claim reserves, whether or not influenced by access to sophisticated databases, are estimates of an insurer's ultimate liability for losses. Insurers monitor the differences between amounts reserved and final payments. They are less concerned that reserves and final payments differ than that the magnitude of the error be consistent over time. Electronic data sources help insurers assess the consistency and error percentage by providing a rapid method to compare reserves with final payments and the ability to assess reserving inaccuracies in different time periods. By identifying trends in inaccuracies, insurers can better assess their confidence in their estimates of outstanding reserves. When insurers more accurately forecast their liabilities for losses, they better define their expected profits and surplus, which aids in planning premium growth and investment strategies.

Monitoring Claim Service

Insurance company managers are concerned about the quality of their claim service for the following reasons:

- Insurers have a contractual obligation to policyholders, claimants, and other insured parties.
- An insurer's growth opportunity depends on its reputation for reliability.
- Regulators monitor financial and service aspects of claim handling.
- Insureds might file lawsuits when they believe they are treated unfairly.

Insurers recognize that insurance customers buy insurance to gain the peace of mind that comes from an insurer's written promise to provide indemnification (and other services) should an insured loss occur. Failure to meet the promise of indemnification would constitute a violation of the insurance contract.

> A **claim diary** is a manual or electronic reminder of necessary follow-up action.

Insurance company managers closely monitor their claim service in many ways. One tool insurers use to monitor service is the **claim diary**, which is a system of managing pending action for each claim file. Diaries are used for both simple and complex claims to establish reminders for claim personnel to take some important action.

To illustrate the use of a claim diary, consider the following example. Suppose lightning strikes a tree, which falls on and damages a building. Although repairs could take many weeks, the loss could be reported to the insurer's CSR with one phone call. Assessment of the damage amount might be completed within several hours of a claim representative's inspection. Once the CSR establishes the claim record and the location is inspected, an initial payment might be made so that repairs can begin. However, the claim is not settled until a final determination of the damage amount is established and payment is accepted by the insured.

To ensure that the damage is repaired and that the insured property is restored to the condition it was in before the loss, the CSR and claim representative will establish, or pend, a diary (sometimes called a suspense or suspended file note) to check on the progress of repairs and to determine payment of additional amounts (if any). That helps ensure that the insurer advances payments for indemnification as needed, and it helps the insurer monitor the building restoration process.

Besides monitoring data that describes the progress of the claim settlement, the diary also permits the insurer to know whether incomplete repairs might affect underwriting acceptability. Insurers usually continue to insure structures after a loss and during the time of repair (and the structure may be insured for losses in addition to those that caused the claim). A damaged building could be less resistant to further damage while being repaired, and debris from the loss, open foundations, and other liability hazards might present new exposures during repair. Consequently, the insurer must verify that repairs are completed in a reasonable time and that the structure is returned to the condition that was acceptable to the underwriters before the loss.

Claim representatives receive a large volume of mail (by conventional postal delivery, express mail, e-mail, fax, and the Internet) each day. In some lines of business, a claim representative may be responsible for well over 100 claims in various stages of investigation and settlement. With that magnitude of claim activity, claim representatives spend a great deal of time reviewing a combination of paper records (for example, receipts for insured expenses, medical bills, and repair estimates) and computer records (for such data as evidence of coverage, limits, deductibles, prior settled claims, other outstanding claims, payments, and reserves for multiple claimants in a given loss).

Since each CSR and each claim representative works on many different claims simultaneously, a system that provides an automatic reminder is very important. For complicated liability losses, for which multiple claimants may incur medical expenses over many years, periodic review of outstanding issues (such as status reports on patient rehabilitation, requests for detailed medical records, inspections, and investigative reports) is essential. In addition, failure to monitor notices of lawsuits and deadlines for filing summons and complaint answers could result in unnecessary legal decisions against the insurer. Setting reasonable dates for follow-up is crucial for verifying that appropriate action is taken within reasonable time limits.

Insurers have long maintained manual diaries to check on the status of claims at specific intervals (typically 30-day intervals such as 30, 60, 90 and 120 days after the initial report of loss). However, since many insurers now use electronic databases to create claim records, the same databases can be used to provide reminders for various future action on claims pending settlement. Furthermore, claim personnel can easily customize electronic reminders for each claim.

In addition, some claim systems use accumulated claim handling data to identify follow-up action typically required for each type of claim. For example, if most homeowners losses with reserves over $10,000 result in payments under the additional living expense coverage of the homeowners policy, the system's diary might suggest follow-up action for obtaining receipts of the insured's expenses associated with temporary living quarters. Systems can both suggest an appropriate type of future action and indicate a reasonable follow-up date whenever claim personnel make an adjustment to a file. Unless the claim person assigns an alternative action or different diary date, the system would automatically define an action and set the follow-up date.

Another data source insurers use to verify adequate service is the claim file documentation process. Whenever claim representatives take some action on a claim, whether reading an item of correspondence, reviewing a bill, conducting a phone call, or sending a message, a written description of that action is made in the claim file. Notations are made each time any information related to the claim is generated, received, or reviewed, whether on paper, by phone, or electronically. Some claim representatives write descriptions in a paper file designated for each claim. Increasingly, however, such notes are entered as data to an electronic claim file. That permits simultaneous access to all of the data in the same file throughout the insurer's electronic communication network.

If notes are made to paper files, the person making the notation must typically establish a follow-up action and pend a reminder in a separate diary system. Such separate systems are sometimes manual but are increasingly incorporated into an electronic communication system. If notes are made to electronic files, the same system that accesses the claim file database usually provides the diary system. Such systems can be programmed to suggest an appropriate next review date based on the insurer's experience with similar claims in similar stages of settlement.

Although claim representatives (or their supervisors) are usually permitted to override automatic diary dates, the availability of such diaries can reduce some of the difficulties insurers encounter when follow-up action must be performed by a deadline. Also, if claim representatives fail to respond to a diary date, the system can automatically refer the diary to another claim specialist or member of claim management for handling. That way, necessary steps or tasks are less likely to be ignored than when manual diary systems are used.

Insurers collect data that reveal the time required to handle each type of claim. Such data provide insurers another method to manage claim service. By knowing how frequently each claim must be reviewed and how much time claim representatives spend on each claim, insurers can determine average time required for claims in each coverage and each line of business. The data can be used to set time standards for each claim type. Some simple claims can be settled in less than an hour, but more complicated losses may require over 100 claim representative hours just to document the extent of injuries for claimants. Over years, data are collected showing the hours required by each claim, and standards can be adjusted when averages change.

Average claim handling time data are also useful in estimating how many claim files of a particular type a claim representative can be expected to handle while delivering adequate service to policyholders and claimants. Measurement is also useful in quantifying the amount of work that might need to be temporarily reassigned when an insurer's number of claim personnel decreases because of reassignment, vacations, resignations, and illness. The process of collecting claim-handling time data also identifies claim representatives who require more than average time to handle losses. Management can then evaluate the reasons for the greater time requirement, reassigning claims or providing training as necessary. Monitoring claim-handling time data electronically (and ensuring that reasonable standards are maintained) helps insurers increase their confidence that customers will be satisfied with the insurer's claim service. Accurate measures of claim-handling time also help insurers demonstrate compliance with regulator standards for required claim response times.

Insurers do not depend solely on electronic data sources to monitor claim service. Since customer perception of insurer service is important for an insurer's reputation as a reliable source of fair claim settlement practices, insurers frequently survey their policyholders and claimants to determine levels of satisfaction. To save on expenses associated with surveying customers, some insurers combine a short customer survey with a letter that accompanies mailed claim settlement checks. Exhibit 3-3 illustrates a sample letter.

Exhibit 3-3
Survey of Customer Needs

Dear:

You recently experienced a property loss that resulted in a claim with Acme Insurance. We are interested in your opinion about the quality of service you received from us. Please take a few moments to help us learn how we might better serve you in the future. You may send your response in the attached envelope, fax this letter to 888-555-1234, or call me toll free at 800-555-5678 with your comments.

Sincerely,

Dana Ford
Customer Service Manager

1. When you contacted us about your recent loss, did we investigate your claim quickly?_____

2. Were you satisfied with our claim service?_____

3. Are you satisfied with our service in general? _____
    _____

4. What would you like to see us do better in the future? _____
    _____

Surveys are useful for assessing customer perceptions. An insurer might learn from surveys that its contact time from the time the customer or claimant reports the loss to when the claim representative phones the insured is faster than that of competitors. However, the insurer might learn that customers perceive a lack of courtesy or friendliness that could cause customers to be disappointed in its claim handling. Similarly, an insurer might receive a compliment for the extraordinary measures taken by a particular employee in accommodating a customer. By collecting such manual data, insurers can gain additional information about their claim service that can be useful in improving service quality, documenting customer perceptions, and recognizing superior achievers. Survey forms can also be designed to facilitate recording results electronically. However, frequently the most useful information obtained from this data source is in the narrative comments some respondents provide.

Payment Processing and Quality Control

Insurers process thousands of claim payments every day. Electronic data management greatly enhances insurer ability to expedite check production and mailing. Claim representatives can specify settlement amounts while reviewing electronic claim files. Supervisors reviewing payment authorizations electronically can review payment recommendations referred instantly and automatically from claim representatives. Accounting departments can process payment requests electronically, often without the need for human involvement. Electronic fund transfers can move payments from insurer accounts to claimant accounts within hours. Consequently, insurers' ability to collect and manage claim data permits many simple claims to be submitted, evaluated, and paid within twenty-four hours of the time the customer or claimant reports the loss.

The same electronic systems that process payments can be designed to verify the reasonableness of payment amounts by comparing data from the requested check amount with the loss reserve data in the claim file and with a predetermined list of value ranges for the particular type of claim payment. For example, a reserve for the replacement of an auto windshield might be set for $500. A subsequent repair estimate after deductible could result in a payment authorization of $375.98. The system might be programmed to compare the payment authorization with the claim reserve from the claim file. In this case, it would find the payment authorization of $375.98 to be close to the reserve amount. The system might also be programmed to compare the payment authorization amount to a value list to verify that the payment requested is below a maximum limit for that type of claim (which, in this case, might be $800). Consequently, those two electronic verification processes would identify a serious mistake, such as a misplaced decimal. The system would prevent a mistake such as a payment of $3,759.80 instead of $375.98 by producing an error warning.

Insurers continue to refine their use of electronic data systems in the claim-handling process while using other sources of data, like customer surveys, to improve their understanding of their service. In addition, insurers contribute loss data to industry-sponsored antifraud and crime detection databases. Special investigative units use industry data stored in these databases to identify suspicious claims and potential fraud. Successful efforts to minimize unjustified loss payments lower insurer loss ratios and could reduce the premium increases that would otherwise be necessary. As insurers gain greater understanding of the potential uses of data they already collect, greater efficiency in the claim settlement process should result.

Information Management Cases

The following two hypothetical cases illustrate how insurers use data to make decisions and to gain advantages in competitive markets. As you read each case, consider which sources of data the insurer chooses to access and monitor, what information is derived from the data, and who should receive the information.

New Product Company

New Product Company (NPC) is a hypothetical direct marketing personal lines insurer specializing in personal auto insurance. NPC has a reputation for offering competitively priced auto liability and physical damage coverage to over 200,000 customers who live throughout the United States. NPC has a reputation for rapid customer response through its toll-free telephone service centers and for prompt and fair claim payments. NPC also seeks to offer innovative product features that it believes will appeal to large numbers of customers and that will generate significant additional profits.

Five years ago NPC responded to customer demand for higher limits of towing and labor coverage by increasing its standard limit to $75 per disablement and offering optional increased coverage of $150. Twenty percent of NPC's customers with towing and labor coverage have purchased the increased limits.

NPC has been considering adding auto warranty service contracts to its portfolio of insurance products. Insurers that offer warranty coverage typically limit its availability to vehicles newer than seven model years old, and owners must elect to purchase the coverage within thirty to sixty days after vehicle purchase. Such coverage is typically subject to a $100 or $200 deductible, and coverage expires when a vehicle accumulates 12,000, 24,000, or 36,000 miles after the effective date of warranty coverage. Many states regulate warranty coverage. Consequently, NPC can access the premium and loss results of warranty coverage.

Industry analysis by NPC reveals that sales of warranty coverage have been highly profitable even with relatively high commissions paid to agents. Since NPC is a direct marketer paying no commissions, NPC management believes the insurer could offer competitively priced warranty coverage. Also, since it communicates with many auto insurance customers shortly after they purchase replacement vehicles, it believes it has an excellent opportunity to sell warranty coverage.

Before members of NPC senior management will approve the introduction of warranty coverage, they want to know how NPC's underwriting, marketing, and claim management will measure the performance of the warranty product. They develop the following series of plans for collecting and analyzing data:

- A weekly plan for expected sales, premiums, losses, and expenses will be defined (made available to management for their decision-making process and, later, to those responsible for comparing actual results with the plan).

- NPC's number of sales, premiums, losses, and expenses will also be monitored daily and compared with the planned results (monitored by sales and claim professionals, processors, underwriters, and management).

- Industry results for similar products will be monitored and compared with NPC's results monthly (typically monitored by management and sales professionals to assess industry trends for comparative purposes and to identify emerging trends).

- A representative group of customers who have purchased the warranty coverage will be surveyed quarterly (usually by marketing professionals to assess customer response, but results will be distributed to all who contribute to the customers' perception of the insurance product, including customer service, claim, underwriting, and sales personnel).

- Trends in claim frequency and severity will be summarized monthly in a report to management to identify territorial differences (distributed to claim and underwriting personnel to identify areas with the most and least loss activity so that causes can be identified and rate and underwriting actions can be initiated).

- Trends in age and type of vehicles insured will be monitored quarterly to identify trends in the profile of customers (distributed to claim, underwriting, and marketing personnel to identify potential problems concerning adverse selection, underwriting guidelines, and pricing).

- Processing time from date of coverage request to written confirmation of coverage to customers will be monitored monthly and compared with average processing times for other products (underwriting, administrative processing, and marketing could all benefit from knowing how promptly NPC responds to customer inquiries).

* Billing/payment receipt processing time will be compared with typical processing times for auto liability and physical damage policies to identify inconsistencies (accounting, marketing, billing, and administrative processing personnel would be interested in comparing how rapidly the insurer bills and collects premium due).

These are examples of the types of data and information that an insurer such as NPC might consider necessary for a new product introduction.

Growth Company

Rapid Growth Company (RGC) sells workers compensation insurance in three states in the western United States. Since workers compensation insurance coverage and rating is established by statute in the states in which RGC operates, RGC cannot use coverage or price to distinguish its products from the products of its competitors. However, RGC has used new PC technology to introduce detailed payroll reporting and analysis software. The data are important to RGC's customers because workers compensation premium rates are a function of the payroll and job classifications for customer employees. RGC's software enables its customers to monitor, on a daily basis, payroll by job classification. It also permits RGC's customers to know how payroll will affect the amount of its workers compensation insurance premium.

RGC provides its software to all of its customers. The software is used to report payroll and job classifications to RGC. (Underwriters verify the reasonableness of payroll and classifications based on payroll audits conducted every year.) Since the software operates on almost any PC, even employers with relatively small computers who have access to the Internet can typically benefit from its use. RGC's program uses point-and-click technology. It is highly user friendly. Besides helping customers report and monitor salaries and job classifications, RGC's computer system links claim data with payroll data and permits customers to access the status of outstanding claims. When a claim occurs, the claim representatives obtain and record detailed loss data, including date of accident, time of day, injury circumstances, personnel involved, witnesses, work activity involved, body parts injured, extent of injury, medical evaluation, prognosis for recovery, medications likely, probable length of disability, and effect on employer loss experience. These data are updated on the employer's computer whenever the employer contacts RGC to report daily (or weekly) payroll amounts.

Large employers have learned how to use the daily information to better manage their work activities. Many have reduced loss frequency by identifying sources of injury and improving employee safety procedures. The increased attention to loss experience made possible by RGC's system helps employers identify jobs and employees that have the most frequent injuries. By directing management attention to those jobs and employees, the information enables supervisors to become more attentive to safety conditions. In addition, the frequency and severity of injuries can be reduced, employees can be encouraged to return to work more quickly, loss ratios are lower, and insurance premiums are less. So although RGC cannot distinguish its workers compensation insurance product by using unusual coverages or rates, its ability to collect data and manage information serves as a significant competitive tool. The following are advantages RGC's data and information might give it over their competition:

- Simplified electronic payroll reporting
- Frequent premium adjustment reflecting actual daily payroll
- On-demand data describing each current and outstanding loss
- On-demand payment/recovery status on every outstanding and paid loss
- Electronic reporting of injuries to regulators
- Ability to sort injury data by dates, job function, employee, supervisor, work location, type of injury, and other classifications
- On-demand assessment of accumulated loss experience and its effect on workers compensation premium
- Mutual access to premium, billing, and loss information that facilitates discussion of discrepancies between customers and RGC
- Readily available detail that facilitates responding to questions from employees, medical care providers, and regulators
- Continuous payroll updating that facilitates RGC's identifying qualified employees when claims for injuries are submitted, which speeds the claim-handling process and payment for services
- Availability of RGC's system at no cost to its customers, which minimizes expenses to employers and reduces the need for independent audit of payroll and loss records

To the extent that employers perceive such access to data and information as a significant advantage, RGC might be a more appealing source of workers compensation insurance than competitors. Systems like RGC's could probably provide other advantages to employers. For now, it is sufficient to understand some of the types of advantages an insurer interested in growth can gain from the effective use of data and information. Those advantages could be of particular value for insurers that sell products that are difficult to differentiate from competitors' products, as is often the case with workers compensation insurance.

Security of Data and Information

Entire texts have been devoted to the subject of managing the security of data and information. This text defines security as a system of safeguards for protecting information technology against disasters, systems failure, unethical use, and unauthorized access that can result in damage or loss to electronic information or to the organization because of dependency on the technology. The following are five components of security:[1]

- Identification of and access by users
- Encryption
- Protection of software and data
- Ethics of data access
- Disaster recovery planning

Identification of and Access by Users

Access to data and information is typically restricted to those who have the appropriate access devices (such as keys to computer rooms; system terminals; and identification cards with magnetic codes, signatures, and badges) and who know the appropriate identification numbers, sign-on procedures, and passwords. Human physical traits like voice characteristics can also be digitally recorded. Electronically recorded physical traits (such as a reading of a hand or fingerprints) can be compared with images assessed by cameras verifying identity. Call-back systems restrict access by establishing linkage only with certain predefined electronic access points, or terminals; an individual trying to access a system from other than that terminal will be prevented from gaining access.

Encryption

Encryption, or **enciphering**, is the altering of data so that the data must be restored to the original condition before the data can be used. Good encryption systems can restrict access by all but the most competent manipulators of ciphering. Frequently, one key is used to input data, and a different key is used to read the data. Use of two keys in encrypting data greatly increases the complexity of decoding the data. Although encryption may be desirable for government and trade secrets and other matters of great confidentiality, effective encoding also permits uninterceptable transmission of illegal data. That capability raises questions about whether the government should regulate who can use encryption in establishing security arrangements for data. Some insurers establish guidelines for the type of sensitive data that warrant encryption so that if the government considers limiting the type of data that may be legally encrypted, the insurer could better defend its use of encryption for specified types of data.

Protection of Software and Data Files

Data files and software are protected in many ways. Data back-up technology, antivirus detection systems, power surge protection, and other techniques are common means of protecting electronic data storage. Records of who accesses certain types of data and for how long are also useful for verifying the security of data. Audit controls are used to track the programs and servers used, to identify which files were opened and in which sequence, and to serve as a trail through user access. Since employees with authorized access to data are the greatest threat to data and information security, the screening of job applicants, including verification of prior employment and references, is essential. Limits of access authority should be defined and enforced according to employee need and level of management confidence in the trustworthiness of each employee to whom access is granted. Access to data and information that is nonessential to job functions is typically restricted.

Errors of input and output can also undermine the usefulness of data. Consequently, security is also a function of data accuracy. Management failure to identify sources of potential error and to ensure that data are evaluated for the possibility of that error can result in contaminated data that cannot be used for the intended purpose. Controls of output documents containing sensitive information can help ensure that data produced in paper form are shredded or otherwise destroyed when no longer needed.

Ethics of Data Access

An emerging issue for insurers is ethical use of information. Public concern about the volume of personal data collected by various entities increases the probability that consumers will demand greater protection from unauthorized use of the data and the information derived from the data.

Consider the detail provided in a typical personal auto insurance application. Besides the possible use of names and addresses for solicitation of other products, other types of demographic information can be derived from application data. For example, the age and type of vehicles listed suggest lifestyle and values. The nature and relationship of household members suggest marketing opportunities for a range of products. Retail credit reports obtained in the process of underwriting applications provide substantial detail about income, payment history, personal preference, and lifestyle. Information about driving habits derived from motor vehicle operator records also suggests personal characteristics.

A study conducted by researchers at the College of Business, Oregon State University (Corvallis) in 1997 titled "Ethical Uses of Information in Insurance" gives a detailed review of the relationship among law, ethics, and privacy; provides guidelines for information gathering; and recommends ways to manage the ethical risks associated with use of information.[2] The study recommends that insurers develop a code of ethics for information use as a way to communicate management's expectations to the employees.

Most insurers require data for the underwriting of insurance products for which the customer has requested coverage. However, the Oregon State research shows that most laws governing privacy apply to government entities only; few apply to private corporations and individuals. Few laws limit the potential misuse of data and information like the type of information insurers collect. The Fair Credit Reporting Act (FCRA) of 1970 requires consumer-reporting agencies to adopt reasonable procedures for meeting the needs of commerce for consumer credit, personnel, insurance, and other information. The FCRA requires that such procedures result in fair and equitable treatment of consumers with regard to the confidentiality, accuracy, relevancy, and proper use of such information.

The National Association of Insurance Commissioners (NAIC) Insurance Information and Privacy Protection Model Act is intended to guide states in establishing privacy statutes. Adopted in seventeen states, it allows consumers access only to information about themselves that is "reasonably described, reasonably locatable and retrievable." The Oregon State research finds that consumers do not own the information gathered about themselves. Dangers that may result from inappropriate use of data collection include the following:

* The large volume and varied types of information may be irrelevant to the primary purpose for which it is gathered.
* Permission is rarely obtained for alternative uses of data and information.
* Information stored electronically tends to be retained indefinitely.
* Individual records may contain significant numbers of errors.
* Access to databases may be inadequately controlled.

Besides threatening privacy, these dangers also present potential problems for insurers, particularly if case or statutory law develops causes of action in tort for alleged violations of rights to privacy. For the present, much of the protection of consumer privacy interests remains a function of an insurer's voluntary ethical practices and professional discretion. Most insurers want long-term access to underwriting information, and that desire is likely to motivate care in their decisions about what data should be accessed and how the data should be used and protected. However, abuses of information by a minority of insurers could result in future regulation for the industry. Insurance professionals may limit the possibilities for abuse if they evaluate data and information access and security from both the insurer's and the customer's perspectives.

Disaster Recovery Plans

Comprehensive disaster recovery plans typically include arrangements for alternative office space, employee notification procedures, key person contact lists, alternative customer response capability, and other arrangements that help the organization continue its operation with a minimum of disruption. Plans typically address disasters caused by such catastrophes as a major fire, flood, earthquake, or hurricane. Organizations that depend extensively on data and information for their business operations, like insurance and finance businesses, face potentially serious disruption if their access to data is impaired, even though their physical facilities might be unaffected. As organizations increase their use of off-site data and information storage and retrieval, they typically address in their disaster recovery planning the interruptions that could occur if the flow of information was impeded for a prolonged period.

Mainframe-based systems are typically operated by systems professionals who are trained in sophisticated precautions to maintain the availability of mainframe data. Insurers often establish alternative data storage and retrieval by using multiple processing centers that might normally process a portion of the organization's data needs but have the capacity to temporarily meet the entire organization's data requirements. However, for data and information stored in PCs, the responsibility for establishing and maintaining comprehensive disaster recovery plans is typically retained by managers whose specialization is in areas other than data and information management. That decreases the probability that adequate disaster recovery planning will occur.

Each organization must determine the extent of an appropriate disaster recovery plan. One way to assess how extensive a plan an organization should have is to estimate the cost in terms of customer service and claim handling if access to current sources of data were eliminated immediately. It has been estimated that a typical company loses as much as 3 percent of its annual gross sales within eight days of a sustained computer outage. It is also estimated that an organization that loses computer capacity for ten or more days never fully recovers the lost revenue.[3] Businesses dependent on electronic data to the extent that insurers are could experience much higher losses, particularly if data supporting defenses of large liability claims are permanently lost. Consequently, the security of insurer data and information deserves substantial management attention.

Systems Thinking

In recent years, management theorists have expressed concern that organizations need to better understand themselves as systems, or operating within systems, rather than just a collection of functions. The concept, often called systems thinking, or holistic thinking, has been thoroughly explained by management writers such as Peter Senge, Tom Peters, and Russ Ackoff. They define a system as existing whenever two or more parts work together to achieve a common goal. In organizations, that typically means two or more employees working cooperatively to achieve a mutually desirable goal.

Holistic approaches to the interaction of parts in achieving results have existed since early Greek and Asian philosophy, so systems thinking is not entirely new. However, during the seventeenth century, science and philosophy began to analyze the parts of various subjects, and a mechanistic view of thinking became dominant. People began to think that they could better understand life by analyzing the components of whole entities. Each part was analyzed in isolation, and the understanding that resulted reinforced the emerging view that people could fully understand their environment by examining its parts. That method of thought, sometimes called mechanistic thinking because it looked at the operation of things as if they were machines, benefited human learning for centuries. It was particularly useful during the industrial age because mechanistic thinking complemented the development of sophisticated machinery and the manufacturing employment it provided.

In the industrial age, most employment was in mass production facilities where the specialized ability of individuals performing repetitive tasks helped organizations achieve high levels of productivity. A mechanistic philosophy helps manufacturing workers perceive their jobs as part of the linear sequence of events leading to the creation of some final product. However, when the product is knowledge, such as is the case for today's insurance and finance products, employees must be capable of identifying data that can be used to create useful information for a wide variety of changing circumstances. Insurance and finance products depend on the effective interaction of many employees acting not necessarily in sequence, but in networks that change according to the need for information. Those networks function more like interdependent systems than like machines.

The increasing availability of data and information made possible by technological advances is driving the desire to expand ability to meet demand for knowledge-based products. Those products depend on the effective interaction of employees who share access to data and information and who can identify and collect the necessary data and interpret the data to access needed information. For knowledge businesses, an organizational philosophy that helps employees make sense of their environment as a network of interdependent individuals is more useful than a philosophy that views workers as unrelated and interchangeable parts in a machine.

One might ask what difference an organizational philosophy makes to an insurer's success. Consider the hypothetical example of Traditional Assurance Company of America (TACA). TACA sells personal auto and homeowners insurance through independent agents compensated by commission. TACA management wants the company to achieve a profit by being a provider of quality, competitively priced insurance products. It seeks to accomplish that goal with its well-defined procedures and operational efficiency. TACA has the following strengths:

- Its agents adhere to underwriting guidelines.
- Its agents provide complete applications.
- Its agents locate and communicate with customers.
- Its underwriters are experienced at uniformly applying underwriting guidelines.
- Its processors make few data input mistakes.
- A computer system produces its policy forms quickly.
- Its rate levels are competitive.
- An independent claim-adjusting firm handles its claims.
- Its employees are compensated according to how well they meet company efficiency standards.

TACA's employees are evaluated on the speed and accuracy of their processing and on the number of applications they can process daily. No exceptions are made to the underwriting and pricing guidelines. No new products are introduced. Employees thoroughly understand their jobs but have little knowledge of any other jobs and little interaction with employees who perform other functions.

TACA is organized according to the functions of underwriting, processing, administration, and claims. Each of these functions has specific responsibilities, and the senior managers of each function report to TACA's president. TACA's operation benefits from a mechanistic philosophy that supports the sequential and noninteractive nature of work performed by its employees. Access to data describing TACA's results is generally restricted to supervisors and managers, who interpret data to decide how instructions to employees should be changed.

When agents, customers, claimants, or regulators pose unusual questions, data are usually needed that are not available to most employees. When that occurs, the knowledge level of the underwriters or processors is usually insufficient for them to respond. Consequently, inquirers must communicate through successive levels of management to locate someone with sufficient knowledge, access to information, and authority to respond. That approach has served TACA for many years.

System Company (SC) is another hypothetical insurer that sells auto and homeowners insurance. SC's management also wants to achieve a profit by offering competitively priced products. However, SC perceives a different set of strengths than TACA does. They are as follows:

- SC solicits customers with direct mail and Internet advertising rather than through independent agents.
- Its agents are salaried CSRs.
- CSRs perform many functions, including
  - Selling insurance policies
  - Entering customer data into the company's computer system
  - Rating and underwriting policies
  - Issuing declarations pages and other policy forms
  - Initiating billing procedures
  - Answering customer questions about premium payments
  - Responding to customer requests for policy changes
  - Receiving first reports of claims
- CSRs are available twenty-four hours a day, year-round.
- Each CSR receives a minimum of ten weeks' concentrated training in accessing data through SC's computer system and in insurance coverage

issues before assuming regular responsibilities. Each CSR is also licensed as an agent or a solicitor.

- Management is organized according to customer geographic location rather than by insurer function.

- Employees and management are compensated according to how well they meet customer expectations.

Most of SC's employees are CSRs who interact directly with customers and claimants. They must know how to access a wide range of information, which is available to them through SC's information system. CSRs must also know whom to contact when a question exceeds their knowledge, such as when an attorney calls with a question about a claim or when a regulator inquires about the handling of a particular policy cancellation. Consequently, SC's CSRs are introduced to senior underwriting and claim technical specialists and profit center managers early in their careers with SC, and they meet weekly with them to discuss questions about pending applications for coverage, endorsements, and new claims.

SC's CSRs are evaluated by supervisors who monitor telephone interaction between CSRs and customers. SC also performs customer service surveys, the results of which are incorporated into CSR performance evaluations. Although CSRs are expected to process a minimum number of transactions each week, CSR evaluations are influenced more by the extent to which they please customers with courteous and correct responses to information requests. Often, CSRs consult with their supervisor, more experienced CSRs, underwriters, or claim personnel to answer customer questions. When customers seek coverage that SC does not normally provide, CSRs try to make reasonable referrals to a list of well-qualified alternative sources of coverage. Customers have come to expect SC's CSRs to answer almost any kind of question related to auto or homeowners insurance.

SC is an example of a company that perceives itself as a system of interrelated functions. There are no underwriting, administrative, processing, marketing, or claim managers. Instead, SC employs profit center managers who are responsible for the sales, service, claim handling, and overall profitability of geographic territories. Profit center managers are compensated based on how well their territory meets the organization's objectives for growth, profit, service, customer satisfaction, employee retention, and expense control. SC is an example of systems thinking. SC is growing rapidly, particularly through its Internet marketing activity.

A detailed study of systems thinking is beyond the scope of this text. However, systems thinking is greatly facilitated by the wide availability of data and information that has become possible with successive improvements in information technology. Systems thinking is increasingly common in organizations that believe that marketing advantages can be gained by (1) providing employees access to data and information and (2) having the ability to form communication networks that facilitate use of that information.

Insurance professionals should recognize differences between organizations that operate with a mechanistic philosophy and those that operate with a systems thinking philosophy. Both approaches can be effective, and hybrid combinations of the two philosophies are also common. Increasingly, however, customers expect prompt service and demand high levels of competency from their service providers. Insurance organizations that depend on narrowly defined employee knowledge and authority for their success may have difficulty delivering the comprehensive service that customers increasingly demand. In contrast, insurers with employees who use informal networks to access a wide range of data quickly are more likely to satisfy their customers and achieve growth. In competitive markets, such as personal lines, businessowners coverage, and workers compensation insurance, an insurer's ability to access data and convert the data quickly into information that customers value may be the key to future success.

Systems thinking may be particularly useful for insurers because of the awareness it provides for the interaction among the insurer's owners, employees, managers, customers, claimants, and regulators. Such an awareness may improve the organization's ability to identify and respond to an insurer's many stakeholders. Members of systems thinking organizations may have improved their ability to recognize their interdependence and to adapt for the benefit of the organization. Unfortunately, although effective systems thinking enables organizations to better respond to change, change may not affect all members of the system uniformly. Also, systems thinking does not necessarily distribute benefits equally. Some changes require the elimination or outsourcing of some parts of the system. Other changes require the development of abilities that some members cannot develop. Consequently, the future of the insurance industry is likely to require employees and managers who have unprecedented levels of flexibility and an ever-increasing variety of skills. More than ever before, continuous learning will be essential.

Technological advances made in the past thirty years have brought greater change to society than occurred in all of recorded history before the twentieth century. That strongly suggests that the rate of change is likely to continue accelerating. Larry Brandon, in his 1996 book *Let the Trumpet Resound*, describes some of the possibilities of the future of the insurance business. After interviewing many insurer senior executives, Brandon concludes that the insurance industry's future success depends to a large degree on its building "learning organizations...skilled at creating, acquiring, and transferring knowledge and using new knowledge and insights to modify responses to the needs of customers."[4]

Summary

Insurers collect data to assist in the operation of the marketing, underwriting, and claim functions. They access data and use information in marketing to help them design products and choose territories and distribution methods. Data and information that underwriters gather help insurers to satisfy regulatory requirements and to evaluate portfolios of risk more easily. The underwriting data and information help to ensure that the insurer will set adequate rates. A claim department's access to comprehensive loss and coverage data could help it to settle claims more quickly, enabling the insurer to distinguish its claim service from that of its competitors.

Insurers that use information and technology effectively are likely to be able to grow more readily than insurers that collect data and restrict its application to traditional uses.

The security of data and information relies on five components:

- Identification of and access by users
- Encryption
- Protection of software and data files
- Ethics of data access
- Disaster recovery plans

Public concern about the volume of personal data collected by organizations such as insurance companies has increased the likelihood that consumers will demand greater protection from the unauthorized use of data and information. For now, protection of consumer privacy depends on voluntary ethical codes and practices implemented by insurers.

The idea that organizations need to better understand the interactions of their various functions is called systems thinking. The wide availability of information made possible by electronic technology allows insurers to encourage greater shared access to information and networking among their employees. This creates the potential for improved customer service and more rapid response to external change.

Future changes in customer expectations promise additional needs for access to data and information and the need for organizations and employees who can continuously learn.

Chapter Notes

1.   Brian K. Williams, Stacey C. Sawyer, and Sarah E. Hutchinson, *Using Information Technology: A Practical Introduction to Computers & Communications* (Chicago, IL: Irwin, 1997), pp. 551-554.

2.   Copies of the Oregon Study are available at no charge by calling the Insurance Institute for Applied Ethics at 610-644-2100, extension 7851.

3.   Williams, Sawyer, and Hutchinson, p. 554.

4.   Larry Brandon, *Let the Trumpet Resound* (Malvern, PA: CPCU-Harry J. Loman Foundation, 1996), p. 190.

Index

Page numbers in italics refer to exhibits.